COUNTRY STUDIES

BRAZIL

Roger Robinson
Series Editor: John Hopkin

Heinemann

Heinemann Library
Halley Court, Jordan Hill, Oxford OX2 8EJ
a division of Reed Educational & Professional Publishing Ltd

OXFORD MELBOURNE AUCKLAND
IBADAN JOHANNESBURG GABORONE
BLANTYRE PORTSMOUTH NH (USA) CHICAGO

First published 1998

00 99 98
10 9 8 7 6 5 4 3 2 1

British Library Cataloguing in Publication Data
    Robinson, Roger
        Brazil. – (Country studies)
        1. Brazil – Social conditions – 1985 – – Juvenile literature
        2. Brazil – History – 1985 – – Juvenile literature
        3. Brazil – Description and travel – Juvenile literature
        I. Title
        981'.064

ISBN 0 431 01404 3 (Hardback)
     0 431 01405 1 (Paperback)

Typeset and illustrated by Hardlines, Charlbury, Oxford OX7 3PS
Printed in Hong Kong by Wing King Tong Company Limited.

Acknowledgements

The publishers would like to thank the following for permission to reproduce copyright material.

p.4 A Tom Van Sant/Science Photo Library; **p.8 A** Network; **p.8 B** Sue Cunningham Photographic; **p.8 C** Julio Etchart/REPORTAGE; **p.9 D, E and F** South American Pictures; **p.12 A** Sue Cunningham Photographic; **p.13 B, p.20 B, C** South American Pictures; **p.23 B** Panos Pictures; **p.24 A, p.25 D** Colm Regan; **p.25 F** Sue Cunningham Photographic; **p.26 C** Latin American Bureau; **p.27 D** Womankind Worldwide; **p.32 B, p.33 C** Network; **p.36 A** Sue Cunningham Photographic; **p.39 E** BANEGAS, Thin Black Lines Ride Again, DEC (Bhm), 1994; **p.41 A** Mark Edwards/Still Pictures; **P.43 D** Tim Nuttall, Network; **p.42 B, p.44 A, p.47 D** Sue Cunningham Photographic; **p.48 B** South American Pictures; **p.51 B** Network; **p.52 A** South American Pictures; **p.53 C** Julio Etchart/REPORTAGE; **p.55 E** South American Pictures; **p.57 E** Network; **p.58 B** Sue Cunningham Photographic; **p.59 D** BBC Education.

The publishers have made every effort to trace the copyright holders. However, if any material has been overlooked or incorrectly acknowledged, we would be pleased to correct this at the earliest opportunity.

Sources for quotations

p.16 A, B, C based on Stephen McCarthy, *In Search of El Dorado*, Trocaire (1996)
p.17 E based on story recorded by Gerborg Meister in Caipora Women's Group, *Women in Brazil*, Latin American Bureau (1993)
p.24 Box C *Fala Favela*, DEC, Birmingham (1991)
p.25 Box D NEAD/Third World Centre Newsletter No.21, Chantal Finney 'Earth Summit – Rio 1992 and beyond' (June 1993)
p.26 Box A CAFOD
p.27 E (first part) Gilberto Dimenstein, *Brazil: War on Children*, Latin American Bureau (1991); (second part) Ana Vasconcelos, 'Proceedings of the first meeting of street girls, Recife' (1989)
p.49 Box D based on Jane L. Collins, 'Agricultural Restructuring in Brazil', *Development and Change*, Vol. 24, p.79 (1993)
p.50 A (Macaxeiros Ranch, Pará State) Lucy Hetherington, 'Dying for land', *Assignment*, BBC 2 (23 November 1996)
p.51 C (Verdun, Parana State) Paul Vallely, *Promised Lands*, Fount, Harper-Collins, Christian Aid (1992)
p.56 Box B based on 'Paulo's story', *Views from Brazil*, Trocaire (1996)

Contents

1 INTRODUCING BRAZIL

A giant nation of extreme contrasts

A Brazil from space

B Europe and Brazil at same scale

0   1000km

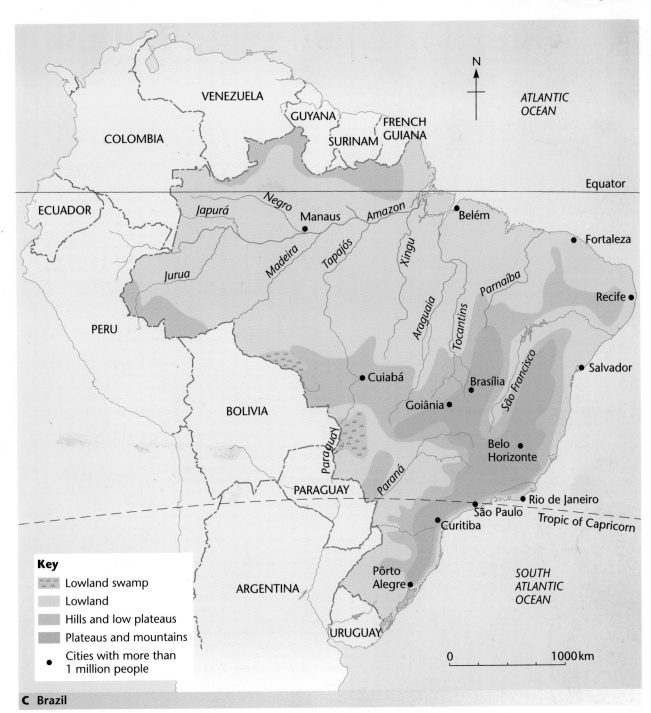

C Brazil

Key

- Lowland swamp
- Lowland
- Hills and low plateaus
- Plateaus and mountains
- • Cities with more than 1 million people

0   1000 km

The area of Brazil is greater than that of the whole of Europe (map **B**), and it has as many people as the UK, France and Germany added together.

Brazil's population has grown dramatically in the last thirty years. The production and consumption of goods have also increased and living standards have risen for many people. Brazil is a nation of huge contrasts – from equatorial forests to temperate grasslands, from flat lowlands to **plateaus** and high mountains, as well as from extreme wealth to terrible poverty.

FACT FILE

The main features of Brazil's landscape can be seen on the 'natural colour' satellite image **A**. The rivers and forests of the Amazon Basin, the dry North East, and the forested hills and mountains all show clearly. The brown colours of the inland plateau area suggest that the thousands of photos used to create the image were all taken during the dry season.

A journey round Brazil

▶ What are the contrasts?

Pete and Cath landed at Recife after a ten-hour journey from London by air via Lisbon costing £870 return each. They were taking a long holiday travelling around Brazil.

The journey is recorded on map **B**. There were seven stages, starting at Recife (A) and finishing at Rio de Janeiro (H).

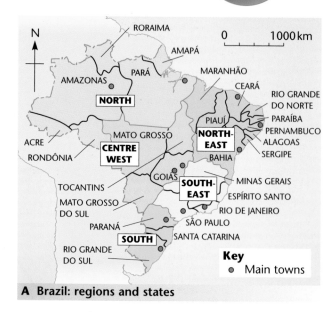

A Brazil: regions and states

Key
● Main towns

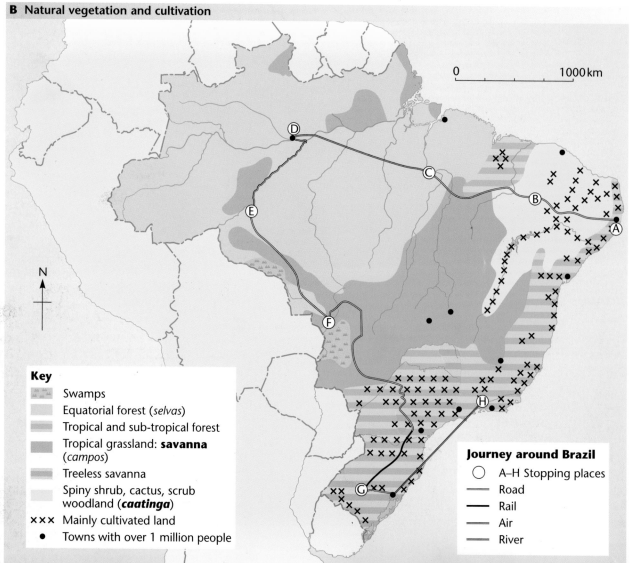

B Natural vegetation and cultivation

Key

Swamps

Equatorial forest (*selvas*)

Tropical and sub-tropical forest

Tropical grassland: **savanna** (*campos*)

Treeless savanna

Spiny shrub, cactus, scrub woodland (***caatinga***)

××× Mainly cultivated land

● Towns with over 1 million people

Journey around Brazil

○ A–H Stopping places

── Road

── Rail

── Air

── River

C Diary extracts

1   Bus, 700km, 14 hours

We spent a couple of days at Recife at a tourist hotel enjoying fabulous beaches. Then we caught a bus inland. What a long journey! For the first hour or so we saw nothing but sugar cane on massive farms, then cattle ranches, then small farms with little roadside houses and neat flowered gardens.
Further inland the ground became stony and dry, and it was very hot. Small plots of beans and maize competed with cattle.
At the small town where we stayed we were told that many people had no land and little paid work was available.

2   Lorry, 1100km, 30 hours

This time travelled on a lorry taking goods to Goiana, though we didn't go that far. Most of the time we were crossing the Mato Grosso plateau lands. Huge numbers of half wild cattle roamed the campos.
Worn out by the travel we stopped off to spend a few days exploring the Panatel - 200 000km^2 of swamps with the most wonderful wild life: birds, parrots, crocodiles, rodents, monkeys, anacondas, fish and countless different plants.

3   Air, 1200km, 4 hours

Sick of buses and cars, we took to the air to Manaus. Endless kilometres of unbroken forest and rivers. Didn't see much of the deforestation once we left the Grand Carajás area. Manaus an amazing town, bigger than I expected.

4   River boat, 900km, 3 days

This was a high spot for me. Luckily the boat was not full and we had space to sleep in hammocks on the deck. Sailing up the River Madeira, through forest and empty savanna lands, stopping at occasional trading posts where Indians sold local produce, was a unique experience.
Pôrto Velho is a modern town, with many people building their own houses or living makeshift. The centre was a bit boring.

5   Land cruiser, 1000km, 24 hours

We got a lift in a land cruiser with a businessman. It was a relief to get out of the arid caatinga area and into wetter parts. Overnight we stayed in an amazing palm forest. Next day it was down into the Amazon jungle crossing giant rivers, to come to Marabá. The businessman took us to see his company's iron ore mines at Grand Carajás - a really massive operation.

6   Bus 250km, 5 hours; air 1200km, 3 hrs

Another bus ride, but luckily Brazilian long distance buses are comfortable and cool. Drove across ranches to fertile coast lands. Caught plane to Rio, a stunning sight from the air - skyscrapers nestled amongst mountains next to the blue Atlantic's bays and inlets. Home tomorrow, what a holiday this has been - but I'm so tired!

7   Bus 1300km, 36 hours; train 600km, 12 hours

Back on the road, many kilometres across the campos again - just high grasses, occasional trees, cattle ranches. This was our longest journey.
Changed to rail after 36 hours. By then we had passed through more fertile lands, subtropical forests and farms, and seen dozens of coffee and sugar farms. Eventually stayed at Santa Maria on the edge of the grasslands where there were cattle, sheep and grain farms. Nearby small farms produced crops like beans, tobacco and rice.

FACT FILE

Size and diversity of Brazil

This journey and the diary extracts demonstrate the size and diversity of Brazil. Each of the five regions contains several states. Some of these states are larger than France, and each has its own state government, working under the umbrella of the National Federal Government.

Pete and Cath see different types of agriculture, and several towns and cities. They use all kinds of transport. The distances involved inside Brazil mean that those who can afford it usually go by air for longer journeys.

Images from Brazil

▶ What would you see?

These six photographs show the variety of landscapes and activities in Brazil.

A Amazon Forest

B The beach at Recife

C Mato Grosso, ranching on **savanna** land

D Coffee *fazenda* landscape

E Farming in the south

F *Caatinga* zone

FACT FILE

Diversity of climate and vegetation

These photos show what it is like in different zones of vegetation and cultivation (see map **B** on page 6).

Photo **A** shows the *selvas*, which has an equatorial climate and covers most of the North Region and Amazon Basin. Photo **B**, of Recife in the North-East Region, is a reminder that the cleared tropical forest lands make wonderful holiday resorts along the coast.

In the tropical **savanna** grasslands of the Centre West Region (photo **C**), a winter dry season reduces the growth of trees. This area is ideal for large-scale cattle rearing.

Photos **D** and **E** show cleared tropical and sub-tropical forests and **savanna**. This farmland is often divided into huge estates – *fazendas* – and is suitable for many crops (coffee, sugar cane, soybean etc.) and fattening cattle. Lands like this are typical of the South and South-East Regions.

The *caatinga* zone in photo **F** is a drought area in the north-east.

History and politics

▶ **What happened in the past?**

▶ **Where are the main areas of economic activity in the 1990s?**

Brazil's long history involves the migration of millions of people, colonization and rapid growth after independence.

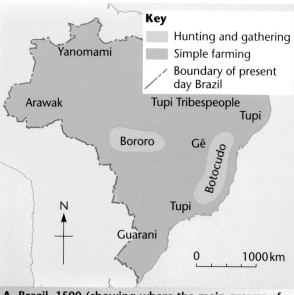

A Brazil, 1500 (showing where the main groups of people lived)

Key
- Hunting and gathering
- Simple farming
- Boundary of present day Brazil

Yanomami, Arawak, Tupi Tribespeople, Tupi, Bororo, Gê, Botocudo, Tupi, Guarani

N

0 — 1000 km

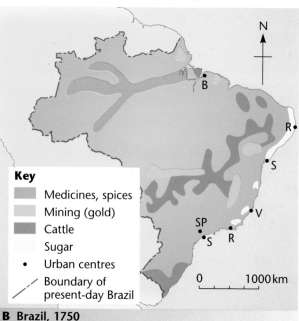

B Brazil, 1750

Key
- Medicines, spices
- Mining (gold)
- Cattle
- Sugar
- Urban centres
- Boundary of present-day Brazil

N

0 — 1000 km

Original peoples arrive, probably from Asia via North America.	3000 BC
Hunting, gathering and simple farming practised by several million Indian people (map **A**).	4500 years
Portuguese colony	AD 1530
First Europeans (mainly Portuguese) colonize east coast. Several million slaves brought from West Africa.	
Bandeirantes (adventurers) blazed trails inland and enslaved native peoples.	300 years
Development of sugar cane plantations, mining (especially gold) and forest products (map **B**); beginning of coffee plantations.	
By **1800** population was 3.25 million, including 1.5 million slaves but only 250 000 Indians.	
Independence – Empire	1822
Many European immigrants arrive on east coast. Portuguese and Italians go to work on coffee plantations; Germans and Polish, as well as Japanese, settle in the south.	70 years
Coffee becomes the most important part of the economy.	
1888 Abolition of slavery.	
Republic	1890
Pioneer farming and settlement fringe pushes across Mato Grosso State and up into Amazon Basin.	100 years
São Paulo and Rio become urban/industrial areas.	
South-east Brazil becomes centre of commercial farming and industry.	
1960 Brasília becomes the new capital city.	
1964–85 Military rule.	
The Brazilian economic 'miracle'. Rapid rise in industrial production and wealth. Even greater differences between the rich and the majority poor. In the interior Indian peoples suffer as mining and farming expand.	
Brazil a regional power and important in the world economy. Internal wealth differences and social problems increase with 1993 world recession and high national debt.	1990s

C Brazil's timeline

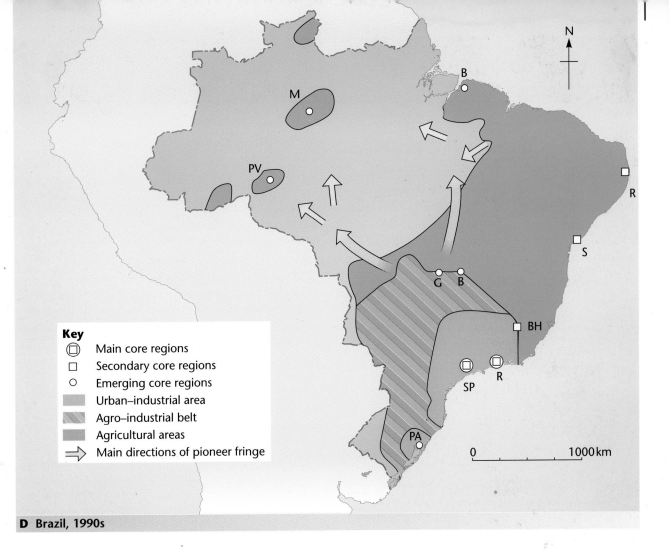

D Brazil, 1990s

Key
- ◉ Main core regions
- □ Secondary core regions
- ○ Emerging core regions
- ▨ Urban–industrial area
- ▨ Agro–industrial belt
- ▨ Agricultural areas
- ⇒ Main directions of pioneer fringe

0   1000 km

Core and periphery in the 1990s

Brazil, like most countries, contains some areas where there is a lot of economic activity, especially industry and business. These are **core** economic regions, where most of the nation's wealth is concentrated.

Away from the cores there are less prosperous **peripheral** areas with less economic activity. Here incomes and standards of living are lower.

Map **D** shows that Brazil in the 1990s has several core regions. It also shows the **pioneer fringe** is still pushing into lands where there are relatively few people or economic activities.

FACT FILE

Colonization

The European colonization experienced by Brazil is quite different to that in Africa. Colonization in Africa was at its height in the nineteenth and early twentieth centuries. By that time the Spanish and Portuguese were well established in South America.

In many parts of Africa, Europeans only settled as traders, administrators and police. The exceptions were the areas with more **temperate** climates like South Africa and the highlands of East Africa. There they settled as farmers, taking over the land from **indigenous** Africans.

Brazil was very sparsely populated at the time of European colonization, and many indigenous peoples were quickly enslaved or exterminated. They were left only in small numbers in environments that were difficult to develop for farming. Needing labour for their farms, the Portuguese imported millions of slaves from West Africa.

People and cultures

▶ How do Brazilians live together?
▶ What have the different cultures contributed?

Brazil has a great variety of peoples and cultures. Diagram **A** shows some of the contributions of the main groups.

Aboriginal Indian groups
- In 1500 there were about five million Indian **aborigines** living in what is now Brazil. Now there are about a quarter of a million.
- Cultural contribution: music, reed flutes, forest crafts and foods.

Portuguese colonists and other European immigrants after 1500
- Portuguese is the official language.
- Roman Catholic Christianity is the religion to which 90 per cent of Brazilians belong.
- Cultural contribution: music, singing, dance.

Slaves, mainly from West Africa
- The **Candomblé** religion has its roots in the Yoruba culture in Nigeria.
- Cultural contribution: music, dance, food.

Recent economic migrants
- These include Europeans (especially Italians and Germans) and Japanese.
- Cultural contribution: music, art, food.

A A Catholic priest blesses a Candomblé follower (Candomblé is a spirit religion different from Christianity; in Brazil it is closely linked to Catholicism)

Mixing the races

There has been a lot of intermarriage amongst the different groups, so that in 1991 over 60 million Brazilians (39 per cent) counted themselves 'mixed' race (table **C**). In spite of this mixing of people there is still racism and inequality as shown in table **D**. Added to this is gender inequality, with women getting half the pay rates of men. What is more, the differences between rich and poor are getting worse. In 1970 the poorest 50 per cent of the nation earned 15 per cent of the national income; now they only earn 10 per cent.

Ninety per cent of the population claim to be Roman Catholic, but many follow forms of religion which are a mixture of Catholicism and the Yoruban Candomblé. The most famous Lent Carnival in the world is held each year in Rio de Janeiro. The climax is the procession of the 'Samba Schools'.

Cultural diversity

Brazilian food, like its people, religion, music and arts, is created from a mixture of cultures. Beans, beef, sugar and coffee are basic ingredients of the national diet. Beans and dried beef with many other ingredients (including chilli) make up the typical *feijoada* main dinner dish. Brazilian rum (*cachaca*) is made from sugar; it is mixed with lime for the *caipirinha* drink. But there is plenty of variety in regional foods. Examples are African dishes around Bahia, and German and Dutch beer brewed in the south.

Apart from the Samba, the Rio Carnival (photo **B**), and the Amazon forests, Brazil must be most famous for its football and the legendary Pelé. In a nation with two-thirds of the people under the age of 29, active sport and evening social activities have a high profile. But, like the rest of the world, television viewing is still the main leisure occupation.

B Rio Carnival

Origins

The cultural diversity of Brazil is mainly due to the arrival of people from different places.

The aborigine peoples probably came to Brazil in prehistoric times from Asia via North America.

Over 10 000 years later the Portuguese were attracted to Brazil by the prospects of land and great wealth. Then, with other Europeans, they organized the slave trade to bring West African slaves to work on their farms and plantations.

More recently, immigrants from Portugal, Italy, Germany and now Japan have been attracted to Brazil in large numbers by its economic opportunities.

Like many other countries, Brazil enjoys the benefits of the contributions of many cultures, but has not overcome racial discrimination.

	1991
European	55
Mixed background	39
African	5
Japanese	0.5
Aboriginal Indian	0.15

C Percentage of Brazilians counted in each group

	% illiterate	Median income (US$ per month)
European (white)	12.2	214
Mixed background	27.9	100
African (black)	30.0	87

D Illiteracy and median income of different groups of Brazilians

2 PEOPLE AND CITIES

Population and change

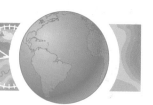

▶ Where do people live?

Change in Brazil has been rapid and dramatic. In 1950 Brazil had a population of about 50 million people, most of whom lived in the countryside. Today there are three times as many people, and 115 million of them live in towns and cities.

While the population grew at 2–3 per cent a year, the nation's wealth grew by more than 8 per cent a year. Brazil became a **newly industrialized country** (NIC) like Taiwan, Mexico and Korea, but much larger than these. Now India and China look set to become even larger industrial giants. Brazil, India and China will soon be global economic powers to rival the USA and Japan.

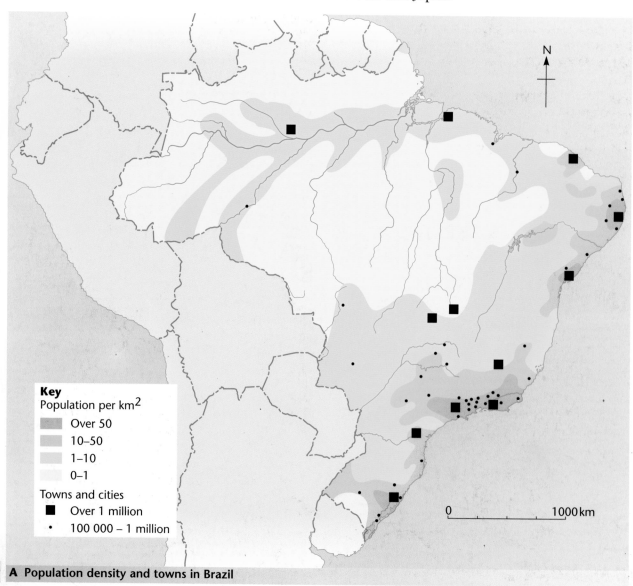

Key
Population per km^2

- Over 50
- 10–50
- 1–10
- 0–1

Towns and cities
- ■ Over 1 million
- • 100 000 – 1 million

0   1000km

A Population density and towns in Brazil

New patterns

Most of the people still live in the south and east (Map A). Population growth is faster in some regions than others (table **B**), and the age structure is also changing rapidly (graph **C**).

	1970	1993
North	3.6	11.0
North-East	28.1	43.9
South-East	39.9	64.2
South	16.5	22.7
Centre West	5.1	9.7

B Population growth in the regions

But the new wealth and development is concentrated into **core** areas (see pages 10–11). People flock to these areas of rapidly growing industries and increase the population of the towns and cities at alarming rates. Many become casualties to **exploitation**, unemployment and housing shortages, though many others make a good living.

City **infrastructure** (transport, water supply, sewerage, electricity) cannot keep pace with the expansion. Even in the core areas a few very rich people have power and an excellent standard of living. The contrast between them and the many poor is huge (diagram **D**).

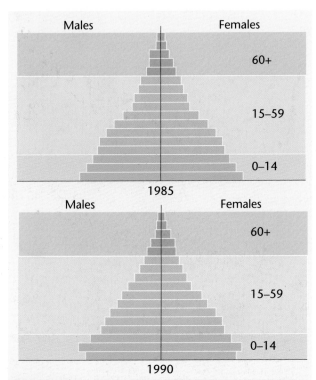

C Changing age structure

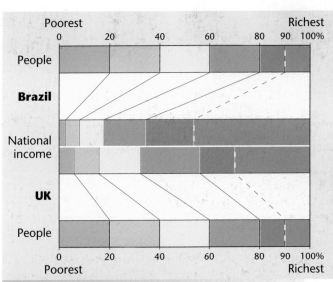

D Distribution of income in Brazil and the UK (each year since 1980 the poor in both countries have been getting a smaller share of the national income)

FACT FILE

Population density

Although Brazil has twelve cities with populations of over a million, the average population density of the country is still quite low. Away from the heartland of the south-east and the east coast, much of interior Brazil has a population density similar to that of mountain areas in other parts of the world.

Brazil is still a country with land and opportunity for people able and willing to withstand the hardships of isolated pioneer life in tropical climates. The North and Centre West Regions contain much of this uncolonized land. Although total population growth in these regions is quite small compared to other regions (graph **B**), the rate of growth is very high. In 23 years the population in the North has grown by 200 per cent, and in the Centre West by 75 per cent.

The rapid increase in population is reflected in the large numbers of young people as well as more people living into old age (graph **C**). But Brazil's population growth seems at last to be slowing down, with fewer children being born in the last five years. This is due not only to family planning, but also to increased economic confidence for many people who no longer feel they have to rely on their children to support them.

Internal migration

▶ **Why move?**

▶ **What are the consequences of moving?**

Internal migration is a feature of all countries. It has always been important in Brazil – today millions of people are on the move from one part of Brazil to another. The never ending stream of arrivals in the cities looking for work and homes, and the struggles for farmland in the interior show how vast this movement is.

There are three main kinds of movement in Brazil:

1   **Migration from rural areas to towns**
    The great urban centres like São Paulo, Rio and Recife are favourite destinations for people from every part of Brazil. All towns, large and small, receive a flow of migrants from the countryside around.

2   **Migration from well-settled areas to new pioneer lands**   The expansion of settlement from the north and east coasts has continued since 1600. New agricultural developments, mining and new transport routes still attract people to the 'frontier' lands in the interior, especially in the Mato Grosso and Amazonia.

3   **Migration from poor regions to richer regions**   This contributes to the other kinds of internal migration, but in particular applies to migration from the North-East Region to São Paulo and Rio.

The stories on these pages describe the lives of some migrants.

Teresa, aged nine, was found dead in the streets of Rio de Janeiro on 22 May 1989, a victim of a death squad.

Teresa's father, Marcelo, had owned a small farm in Pernambuco State. He was pressurized by *pistoleiros* to sell up to the neighbouring sugar plantation owner who needed more land. The family used most of the money to move south on a 50-hour journey to Rio in 1988. They eventually built a small wood and cardboard house in a *favela*. They were without work so Teresa and her brothers had to go out onto the streets looking for odd jobs and begging. Teresa joined a street gang.

A   Teresa

Avelino's family had a small farm for many years, but lost their right to the land in the 1960s.

In 1972 Avelino was given 100 hectares of jungle alongside the Trans-Amazonian Highway in the government scheme to colonize Amazonia. His five brothers and sisters were also given plots and between them they have a large successful farm with a variety of land to grow different crops. They specialized in peppers. Now Avelino is a leader in the local Rural Union which looks after the rights of small farmers.

B   Avelino

Elias was born in Rio Grande do Sul, but his father's farm was too small to share amongst his nine brothers and sisters. Elias qualified for a land grant in Rondônia when in 1968 it was opened up by the Cuiabá – Pôrto Velho Highway. But Elias had difficulty clearing his land and making a living, and after some years was forced to sell to a rancher. So in 1982 he went to the open-cast gold mine at Serra Pelada. He joined 20 000 workers digging by hand in mud pits. The conditions were terrible. He soon gave up and rejoined his family, who had moved to São Paulo after he had sold the farm.

C   Elias

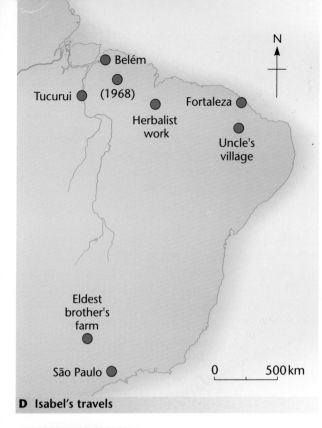

D Isabel's travels

E Isabel's life

Born 1946 in Fortaleza, tenth child, family has no room or resources to bring her up

Move 1 To uncle's village for childhood.

Move 2 Back to Fortaleza for education, but family row over brother's marriage.

Move 3 (1968) To small town in Pará State with her brother and his wife. Has many jobs helping families, exploited as 'slave' labour, becomes sick.

Move 4 Back to Fortaleza by free Brazilian air force flight from Belém. No consistent work.

Move 5 (1974) To São Paulo, lives with relatives, gets poorly paid work.

Move 6 To rural area in São Paulo State where her eldest brother is working. Works with nuns.

Move 7 To a village in Maranhão State with her brother's family to work on an uncle's farm. Worked as a herbalist with nuns.

Move 8 Back to São Paulo, travel paid by uncle. Lives with relations, suffers deep depression.

Move 9 (1977) Back to Fortaleza to work for the church in surrounding rural areas.

Move 10 (1978) Back to original uncle's village near Fortaleza. Involved in trade union work, many quarrels.

Move 11 (1987) To Tucurui Dam in Pará State where her brother worked, but no visitors allowed to stay.

Move 12 Moves back to São Paulo, still no work.

Move 13 To Fortaleza, stays with relatives.

Move 14 To uncle's village where she was brought up, staying with relatives, no secure job.

FACT FILE

Brasília Teimosa, Recife

Across the estuary from the city centre of Recife lies Brasília Teimosa. In the 1930s silt dredged from the river was dumped here and it became dry land. In 1940 a colony of fishermen settled on the land.

In 1950 new migrants from the rural hinterland began to invade. The police were called in. Repeatedly they destroyed the migrants' mud and straw huts; repeatedly the migrants built them again. The fisher people eventually joined forces with the new migrants and the Mayor of Recife withdrew the police.

Between 1958 and 1978 the 40 000-strong community fought off proposals which included a yachting marina and luxury hotels. Self-improvement schemes created mothers' clubs, a residents' council, a school, a theatre group, health centres and a fishermen's cooperative.

Legal ownership was eventually granted in 1989. Since then the streets have been surfaced, housing has been improved and mains water brought to every house.

Urbanization

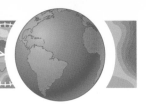

▶ Why move to cities?

The twentieth century has seen the growth of towns all over the world, with the proportion of people living in towns increasing every day. This process is called **urbanization**. In the UK and much of Europe this process took place mainly in the nineteenth century following the Industrial Revolution.

In Brazil rapid urbanization has taken place in the twentieth century. By 1930 a third of Brazilians lived in towns, now over three-quarters do. São Paulo (seventeen million) and Rio (eleven million) are two of the world's largest cities. Belo Horizonte, Pôrto Alegre, Recife, Salvador, Fortaleza, Curitiba and Brasília all have populations of two million or over. Each region has its own giant city.

Most early towns in Brazil were on the coast to provide the link between the productive farmlands and Portugal. So towns like Recife (map A), Salvador, Belém, Rio and Pôrto Alegre grew up as centres of trade, religion and defence.

Inland, mining centres like Belo Horizonte in Minas Gerais State grew up. Belo Horizonte was the first planned town in Brazil (1898) with a regular grid of streets and **boulevards** surrounded by a ring road. Agricultural towns like São Paulo and Curitiba, and the new planned capital Brasília, also developed in the interior. These and the coastal towns grew into the giants of today.

In the early twentieth century growth followed European patterns of suburbs spreading out from one main centre. Recently the cities have followed the US pattern of building whole new areas in cities with their own main centres. These are called **urban realms**.

At the same time the planners and developers have had to cope with shanty settlements growing up on any unused land. So strong contrasts between adjacent rich and poor areas are common in Brazilian cities.

A Recife and new settlement

Key

- Already occupied
- New settlements
- – – – Recife municipal boundary
- ——— Recife metropolitan boundary
- === Main roads

To Fortaleza

City centre — Olinda

RECIFE

To Petrolina

Cabo

To Salvador

N

0   5km

	% of total spending
Housing and urban development	36.3
Administration	14.5
Education and culture	19.7
Welfare and social assistance	9.3
Health and sanitation	4.5
Transport	10.3
Legislature and judiciary	3.3
Agriculture	0.5
Industry, commerce and services	1.0
Employment	0.6

B Spending by Recife **municipality**, 1991

Why people move to towns

Often people have little choice in life and are forced to move (see pages 16–17). Some of the possible forces and reasons contributing to decisions to move to towns are listed in diagram C.

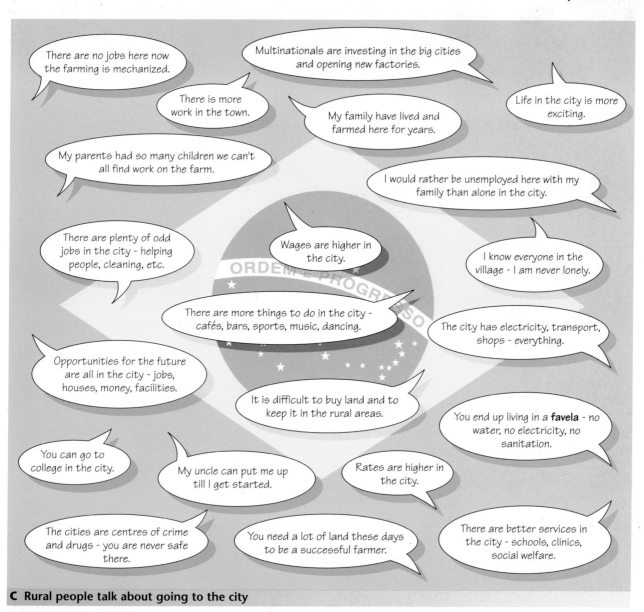

C Rural people talk about going to the city

FACT FILE

Cities

Population 1991		
São Paulo	15 199 423	(now 17m)
Rio de Janeiro	9 600 528	(now 11m)
Belo Horizonte	3 461 905	
Pôrto Alegre	3 015 960	
Recife	2 895 469	
Salvador	2 472 131	
Fortaleza	2 294 542	
Curitiba	1 975 615	(now 2m)
Brasília	1 596 274	
Belém	1 334 460	
Manaus	1 162 316	
Goiania	just over 1 000 000	

The modern phenomenon of mega-cities is not limited to Brazil. Cities in the industrialized world (e.g. New York, Tokyo) are still growing, but even faster growth and larger cities are found in other parts of the world where large rural populations are attracted to the opportunities of the city. Mexico City, Bombay and Shanghai are examples of such mega-cities, and soon it will be Lagos, Nairobi and Johannesburg.

Brazilian metropolitan regions with over one million inhabitants

Two great cities: 1 Rio de Janeiro

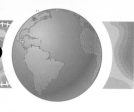

▶ How does landscape and location affect development?

Rio de Janeiro (map **D**) is a global city. Box **A** describes its early development and growth. Photos **B** and **C** show Rio today.

Rio is built on a mountainous indented coast. Governments have tried all kinds of developments – removing hills, filling in parts of bays and cutting motorways through the hills.

Working class districts cluster around the port area to the north, and dozens of shanty towns (*favelas*) are scattered on any steeper slopes or derelict land.

The centre is full of life and skyscraper office blocks and there are some famous beaches like the Copacabana. But the rich have moved far out to new affluent areas to the south of the city.

B Rio: *favelas* and high rise blocks

1 Rio de Janeiro began in the sixteenth century as a sugar mill centre peopled mainly by slaves from West Africa.

2 When gold was found inland from Rio, in Minas Gerais, the Portuguese moved their colonial capital from Salvador to Rio as a better entry port to the interior.

3 In 1822 Rio became the capital of independent Brazil, the port boomed, and industry and business grew. In the nineteenth century, the city was the cultural, business and political centre of Brazil. By 1900 the population was over a million.

4 In the early twentieth century urban renewal transformed Rio from a Portuguese style colonial city into a modern city with different areas for different land uses and a better transport **infrastructure**. The social classes became segregated.

A The beginnings and growth

C Rio: Sugar Loaf Mountain and Botofogo Bay

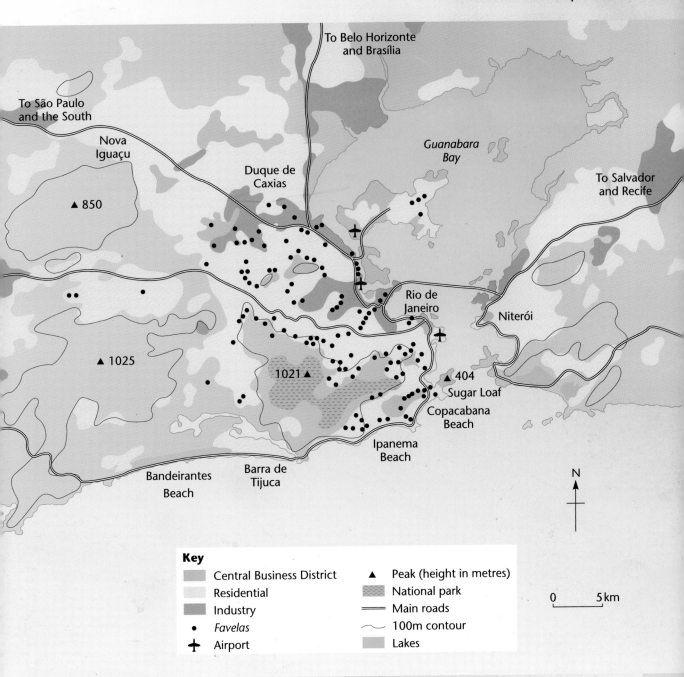

Key

■ Central Business District	▲ Peak (height in metres)
■ Residential	▨ National park
■ Industry	══ Main roads
● *Favelas*	∼ 100m contour
✈ Airport	■ Lakes

0   5km

D Rio de Janeiro

FACT FILE

Rio the beautiful

Rio is famous not only for shanty towns on its hillsides. The Brazilian Embassy describes a different side to this city of contrasts:

Rio de Janeiro has a majestic beauty, with built up areas nestling between a magnificent bay and dazzling beaches on one side, and an abruptly rising mountain range, covered by a luxuriant tropical forest, on the other.

Rio's cultural life is intense and varied. It is in the pursuit of leisure that Rio is outstanding. With its world famous beaches free to all (such as Copacabana and Ipanema), its splendid bay, and its wonderful climate, a blend of summer and springtime, Rio de Janeiro is a city that lives in and for the sun.

Two great cities: 2 São Paulo

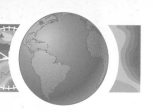

▶ How does a city grow to such a size?

Early days

São Paulo is an example of a city that developed in a similar way to European cities before 1950. São Paulo first grew into a city because of the coffee trade. In 1911 the city was **redeveloped** to make way for road and railway building. It became the transport and trade centre of the region. Industries and business expanded in the city.

Mid twentieth-century growth

By 1950 the rich residents, who had lived near the centre on the Avenida Paulista, were moving out to attractive higher land a little to the south-west. Avenida Paulista became a second Central Business District, especially for banking and business. Most of the retail trade remained in the original CBD.

Industry and workers' housing developed along the main road and rail routes and along the valleys of the rivers Tietê and Tamanduatei, where land was cheaper and less attractive. Large working class housing districts were built there.

The beginning of the car industry

In 1956 the Brazilian government decided to make São Paulo the centre for the car industry. Automobile multinationals sited their factories to the south-east and new working class suburbs grew up. More business was attracted, and a constant stream of migrants came from Europe for work. Shanty towns began to sprout up on empty land inside the city and on the outer edges, especially to the south and east. They are still growing today.

A São Paulo

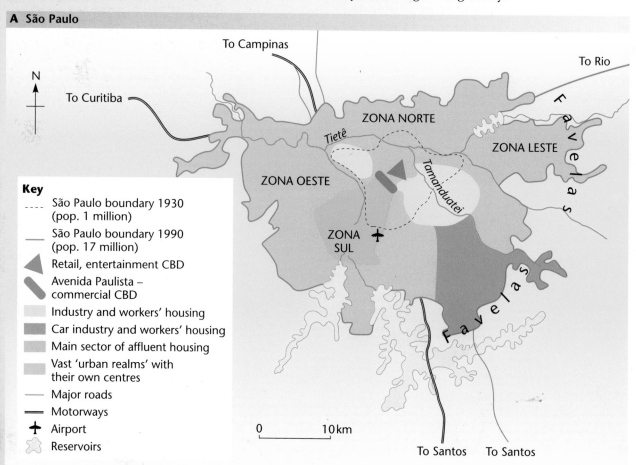

Key
- - - - São Paulo boundary 1930 (pop. 1 million)
───── São Paulo boundary 1990 (pop. 17 million)
Retail, entertainment CBD
Avenida Paulista – commercial CBD
Industry and workers' housing
Car industry and workers' housing
Main sector of affluent housing
Vast 'urban realms' with their own centres
── Major roads
━━ Motorways
✈ Airport
Reservoirs

To Campinas
To Rio
To Curitiba
ZONA NORTE
Tietê
ZONA LESTE
Favelas
ZONA OESTE
Tamanduatei
ZONA SUL
Favelas
0   10km
To Santos   To Santos

B São Paulo city centre

American style

Since 1950 São Paulo has grown in a North American style. There are five **urban realms**. Zona Sul is the richest, with **garden city** neighbourhoods. The city's policy has been to **decentralize**, moving business out into the urban realms. There are fifteen important retail centres outside the CBD and a new business, retail and leisure centre has been built at Berrini, eight kilometres from Avenida Paulista.

But while money is directed to ultra-modern commercial developments, there are still three million people living in single room dwellings, at least another 1.5 million in 2500 *favelas* and half a million on the streets. You can read about some of the results of rapid urban growth in São Paulo in 'Informal settlement' (pages 24–5).

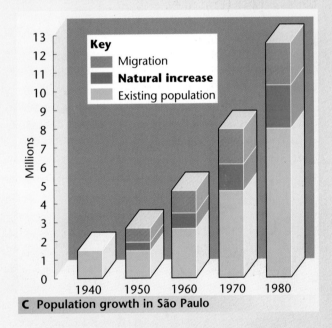

C Population growth in São Paulo

Key
- Migration
- **Natural increase**
- Existing population

Millions (vertical axis 0–13)

Years: 1940, 1950, 1960, 1970, 1980

FACT FILE

The poor

Money is being spent to improve the living conditions of the poor in São Paulo. In 1994/95 the **municipality** invested US $227 million on a programme 'to solve the *favela* problem'. Now they hope to borrow $157 million for projects based on a system from Singapore to build blocks of small flats on *favela* sites (the Cingapora Project). But the project will only house 42 000 people (2 per cent of the *favela* population) and will mean demolishing homes while building goes on.

Unfortunately the position of the poor is not improving in Brazil as a whole. In 1990, 39 per cent of families were below the poverty line. By 1995 the figure was 47 per cent (640 000 families). The ratio of the poorest incomes to the richest was 1:21 in 1990; in 1995 it was 1:31.

Informal settlement

▶ How does rapid town growth affect people?
▶ How can people help to improve conditions in the *favelas*?

It is very difficult to keep pace with urban growth in Brazil. In the last ten years over six million people have migrated to Brazilian cities from the countryside.

Recent migrants often build their own houses on unoccupied land, as a stepping stone to better things in the future – and most of them do either improve their property or move to better areas.

Building temporary shelters is one thing, but providing the necessary urban **infrastructure** is another. So roads, water, electricity, sanitation, schools and clinics all lag behind. In São Paulo less than half the households have drains, and less than three-quarters have piped water. The infant mortality rate has almost doubled in the last fifteen years. But well-organized Self Help Work Groups are now springing up in the *favelas* to tackle these problems.

B PORTO VELHO

Pôrto Velho is a large town in Rondônia State. Almost everyone in Pôrto Velho is a migrant looking for a better life. Many live in temporary shelters while they collect materials to build a house.

Ciudad de Lobo started as a squatter settlement in 1984. The owner eventually gave up trying to clear the squatters and gave the land to the council. Since 1986 a community association has been fighting for services for the area.

C VILA PRUDENTE

Vila Prudente is a *favela* in São Paulo (photo **A**). It began in the 1940s and its residents have fought many hard battles for land, water, sanitation and electricity.

Dona Carmelita lived in Ceará State in the north of Brazil, three days' bus journey from São Paulo. She and her husband and seven children scraped a living from a very small farm on poor land. Her eldest son came to São Paulo when he was sixteen, found a job as a petrol pump attendant, and after two years got his mother to visit him.

Dona Carmelita persuaded her husband and the other children to come to São Paulo and they moved into her son's two-roomed house in Vila Prudente. She worked as a cleaner in an office at night, and looked after *favela* children during the day. Seven years ago she bought a house quite cheaply in the *favela*. She likes living there and is involved with Catholic groups in the community who are trying to improve conditions in the poorest areas. She feels that when people come together many things are possible.

A Vila Prudente

D Interior of a home in Vila Prudente

F A *favela* on a Rio hillside

E A WALK UP THE HILL IN RIO

I go to Andarai, one of the smaller, oldest *favelas*. At first my impression is of well-kept and permanent, though crowded, housing.

We go round with the leaders of the community, Jurema and Odeliea. 'The women are in charge here', they joke. It's through the community association that they have electricity and other improvements like a kindergarten.

Some of the recent improvements are due to the **municipality's** efforts to smarten up the area for the Earth Summit [international conference]. But, as we slowly make our way uphill, conditions worsen. Some of the housing is near collapse; some children are locked inside while mothers are at work; open sewers run down gullies.

Tongue in cheek they call themselves 'environmental criminals'. They are destroying the forest further up the hill for fuel and building materials. They know it increases the chance of flood and landslides, but they have no alternative.

FACT FILE

Favela reactions to redevelopment

Maria Cursi *favela* in Zone Leste of São Paulo has 432 families. It includes 26 small-scale businesses and many door-to-door sales persons and street sellers. Many of the residents are retired with no income.

The people of Maria Cursi voted almost unanimously against the Cingapora Project (see page 23). Rehousing would create many problems for them:

- There would be no guarantee of re-housing once existing houses had been destroyed.
- All businesses in the *favela* would be destroyed.
- At present most *favelados* own their property and have no rent or mortgage.
- To obtain a flat people would have to have registered employment and income.

People in Maria Cursi have other ideas for investment: upgrade their houses; provide clean water, sanitation and electricity; improve roads and pavements. They need facilities like crèches, nursery schools, a community centre and clinics. They also want to participate in decisions about the *favela*.

(Source: Colm Region, *Maps of Exclusion*, 80/20, 1997)

Children in Brazil

▶ **What are the opportunities for young people?**

The general picture

Fifty-five million of Brazil's population are aged under sixteen. Most of these live happy lives in secure families, but seven million are engaged in child labour – 3.5 million of them under the age of fourteen. About 70 per cent of them earn only US $50 per month; others work in semi-slave conditions and receive no wages.

Many respectable companies do not know what conditions exist in the workshops or farms that supply them. Examples of work where children are used include:

- working in furnaces which provide charcoal for the steel industry
- harvesting sugar cane to produce alcohol (an alternative fuel for cars)
- working in shoe industries using highly poisonous glues
- harvesting oranges which are used by multinational companies to make juice.

The economic slump of the early 1990s had its greatest effect on the poor families of children like these (table **B**).

	1980	1991
North-East Region	10.6%	26.4%
Rural South-East	7.9%	25.2%

B Young people in Brazil hit by the recession – percentage of people under seventeen years of age living in families earning up to US $50 per month

Where there are crèches and nurseries, this can help families to deal with the problems of having to work and bring up children at the same time (box **A**).

Street children

Latin America has one of the worst records for abuses of children's human rights. Street children are often seen as a scourge that should be swept away. Killings of children are common, especially by organized death squads (photo **C**). For example, in spite of government promises, in the first three months of 1991 300 young people were murdered in eleven cities.

A A LIFELINE

Several kilometres out in Rio's sprawling suburbs the sign on the crumbling wall said 'The community crèche for a new future'. Inside about twenty under-sixes careered around a dirt yard and queued up to take turns on a plastic see-saw, slide and swing, all given by a nun living nearby.

Joanna runs the crèche. Twenty years ago she had to lock up her young children at home while she sold clothes door to door. To help other women she suggested the crèche to a local community association. It was started with the help of a French priest and donations from locals. They are lucky to have some support from an aid group in London as well.

C A child lies dead on a Rio street

D Ana Vasconcelos, The Passage House, Recife

It is not all bad news. Many small organizations are working with street children to help them to survive, receive an education, get off drugs and eventually lead a normal life (photo **D**).

There are estimated to be seven or eight million street children in Brazil, and 500 000 under-age prostitutes. The stories give some idea of the problems (box **E**).

FACT FILE

'Futures' from a youth group in Rio
Probable future: rich countries richer; more corruption; more unemployment; more unity among the poor; more street children; less health care for the poor.

Preferred future: politics without corruption; workers share profits; farmers own land; fairer prisons; justice for all; proper houses; jobs; no street kids; roads tarred; more solidarity.

How to make it happen: freedom of the press; workers' rights; First and Third Worlds linked as equals; women and men building a better world; kicking out the World Bank and debt.

(Source: *Young People Imagine*; DEFY, Dublin, 1995)

'On the street it's better than at home,' says a ten-year-old girl who sleeps on the steps of the municipal theatre in Rio. 'Here, if you want money, you arrange it, that's life.'

An eight-year-old who lives in a children's refuge called the Boys' Republic says 'I live here because my stepfather doesn't like me. He drinks rum and rows with my mother. He used to hit me, pull my arm, pinch me. Here it's good.'

Beto, aged fourteen, used to work crushing cardboard, now sells sweets and fruit at traffic lights. Sleeps on the street, runs from the police, sniffs glue. Philosophy: share with friends. Hit or run away from enemies, depending on their size.

The Passage House to a refuge for young prostitutes (photo D).

'I know the street has nothing to give. Only beatings. That's why I sniff glue, I don't feel anything.' (fourteen-year-old)

'How can I speak about my life, when they beat me up so that I won't speak?' (eighteen-year-old)

'We are on the street. We are going where we can. We are already dead.' (thirteen-year-old)

E Street children's stories

3 ENVIRONMENT AND RESOURCES

Ecosystems

▶ **How does the climate affect living things in Brazil? What effect has human activity had on the ecosystem?**

Brazil is such a vast country that it has several different types of climate within its borders. Each of these, combined with relief and soils, can create its own natural **ecosystem** with particular animals and plants depending on each other.

The climate changes from equatorial in the north, through tropical, to warm **temperate** in the south. Annual rainfall totals vary from under 250 to over 3000 millimetres. Map **A** and graph **C** show the pattern.

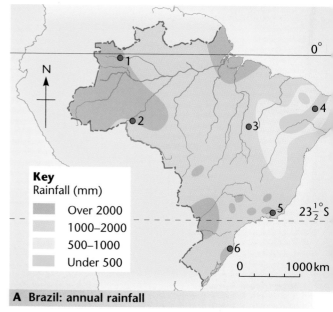

Key
Rainfall (mm)

- Over 2000
- 1000–2000
- 500–1000
- Under 500

$0°$

$23\frac{1}{2}°S$

0   1000 km

A Brazil: annual rainfall

B The rain forest, equatorial climate

Giant trees breaking through canopy

Upper canopy level
Spreading branches form a continuous layer, with many plants growing amongst them.

Lower canopy level
Smaller trees: some young trees just growing up, some full size smaller species.

Bottom level
Small trees and shrubs, seedlings and herbs. Rivers cutting through allow light in and dense plant growth on banks.

50

Metres

40

30

20

10

0

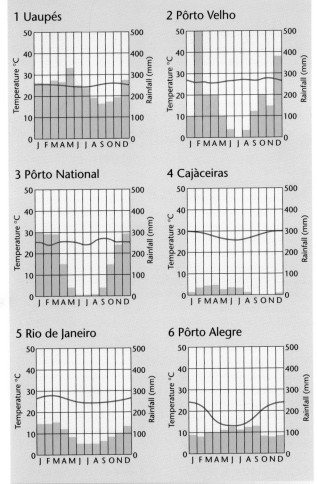

C Annual rainfall and temperatures in six Brazilian towns (see map **A** for locations)

	Number of species	Brazil's position in the world
Mammals	428	3rd
Birds	1 622	3rd
Reptiles	467	4th
Amphibians	516	1st
Butterflies	74	4th
Plants	55 000	1st

D Diversity of species in Brazil

Bio-diversity

Brazil is the greatest store of different living things in the world (table **D**). This is mainly because it has two-fifths of the world's remaining rain forest concentrated in Amazonia (diagram **B**).

Human impact

The effect of agriculture, settlement and industry on natural ecosystems is dramatic. Some parts of Amazonia and the Mato Grosso are still almost 'natural', but human activity now plays an important part in most ecosystems in Brazil. In the south and along the east coast agriculture dominates and creates the landscape. Crops, farm animals and humans all contribute to the water cycle, carbon cycle and nitrogen cycle which are vital for life.

In Amazonia exploitation and human settlement are still at an early stage. The forest is cut and burned to make transport routes and develop farming. This is damaging because it reduces the global bank of species. Burning releases carbon that was previously stored in the trees, sending carbon dioxide into the atmosphere. The industrialized countries, worried about the **greenhouse effect**, have tried to persuade Brazil to control the release of carbon. However, Brazil argues that its contribution to the global problem should be seen in perspective (table **E**).

	Million tonnes
By land use and vegetation:	
World	1659
Brazil	336
By burning fuel:	
World	5000
Top 21 industrialized countries	4077
including:	
USA	1135
UK	141
Brazil	41.5

E Amount of carbon dioxide released per annum, 1980s

FACT FILE

The real rainforest

A visitor describes the Amazonian rainforest:

The trees are particularly high on the flood plains. The fact that the land is covered with water for over four months of the year and the lack of sunlight stops the growth of underbrush. Every tree fights to reach the sun's rays, and the branches and leaves form a solid cover at the top of the forest. The light filters dimly through the forest roof, and the jungle floor remains in half-light, cool and damp. But as one leaves the flood plain, the trees become lower, though still enormous by most foreign standards, and the penetration of sunlight allows the growth of thick underbrush. This is the more typical Amazonian rainforest, less majestic than along the river banks, but more resistant to people.

(Source: adapted from Y. Murphy and R.F. Murphy, *Women of the Forest*, Columbia University Press, N.Y. 1974)

Environmental change and hazards

▶ What creates environmental hazards in Brazil?
▶ What are the costs to the environment and the people?

Natural hazards

Most of the environmental hazards and disasters faced by people in Brazil seem to be the direct result of human activity. Only the severe droughts that hit north-east Brazil can be classified as a truly natural hazard.

The north-east is a dry zone anyway, and farmers are used to water shortage. One problem is that many of them have very small farms and cannot build up savings to see them through bad times. Farm labourers have low wages, and cannot survive periods of unemployment easily. So when a severe drought comes and the summer rains fail, many suffer.

In 1877 some two million people starved to death. In 1985 one million abandoned small farms and migrated. In 1993 six or seven million people were only saved by government 'cash for work' schemes, constructing public roads and buildings. It has been suggested that money might be better spent improving farming techniques to help survive droughts.

In Amazonia the annual floods, which could be a hazard, have been part of life for **indigenous** peoples for centuries. Their farms on the river flood plains (called the *Varzea*), rely on new fertile silt being deposited each year.

A HEAVY RAIN AND LANDSLIDES IN RIO

1966 1000 died when 300 000 cubic metres of debris moved down hillsides.

1967 1700 died and power was disrupted by mud flows.

1988 200 died and 20 000 were made homeless by landslips in *favelas*.

B TUCURUI

Tucurui on the River Tocantins supplies electricity to the Grand Carajás programme (pages 58–9). The flooded land included Indian reserves and 800 indigenous people had to be removed. Some 15 000 other Brazilians were displaced from towns and villages. The rotting vegetation of the drowned forest in the reservoir is polluting the water. Farmers downstream from the dam complain of loss of soil fertility. This is because the *Varzea* is no longer flooded each year and given a new layer of silt.

Human interference

The expansion of farming and settlement bring particular dangers in tropical areas. Heavy rainstorms wash away exposed top soil and deposit it where it is not wanted. Deforested steep slopes are at risk from landslides and mud-flows. Settlements as well as farmland can suffer (box A).

C Completed and planned dams in Amazonia (73 in total)

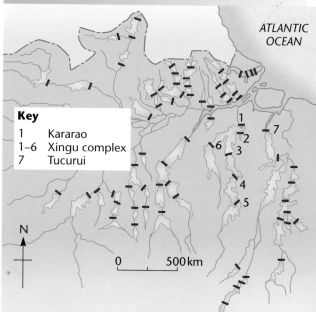

ATLANTIC OCEAN

Key
1   Kararao
1–6   Xingu complex
7   Tucurui

N

0   500 km

In some places, for example Amapá State, open-cast mining has stripped huge areas of vegetation and polluted rivers. The vast reserves of minerals in eastern Amazonia – iron ore, bauxite, manganese and kaolin, for example – attract more investment every year as Brazil becomes more industrialized.

Floods for energy

The drive for hydroelectric power (HEP) in Brazil has led to some of the largest schemes in the world, each flooding many square kilometres of land behind the dam. The Itaipu Dam on the River Parana in the south was seen as a model for development. The local environment was protected, trees planted, and local people (mainly Indians) had their way of life, if not their homes, preserved. But other projects are not so environmentally or socially successful. Amazonia is the focus of development, and it is the indigenous groups that are suffering most (boxes **B** and **E**, maps **C** and **D**).

D The Xingu complex

Key
Legal } Indian lands
Claimed }
Areas to be flooded
Proposed dams

E THE XINGU COMPLEX OF SIX DAMS

The series of dams being built here are creating the problems of Tucurui in another area. The territories of 35 000 Indians will be affected (map **D**). The town of Altamira will be partly flooded, displacing 17 000 people. The first dam, Kararao, is expected to be ready in 1999.

A combination of **environmentalists**, **ecologists**, human rights activists, indigenous people and local immigrants are putting pressure on the government and its electricity company to consider how the project can be carried out with the least damage to the environment and local people.

FACT FILE

The Balbina Dam

The dam on the Uatuma River has created a massive lake of over 2000 square kilometres. Far fewer animals were rescued than at Tucurui. The reservoir not only has the same problems as Tucurui, but has also become a breeding ground for malarial mosquitoes and other diseases.

Some 300 kilometres downstream people are affected by changes in the river. It has been polluted and the flow is much less. It can no longer be used as a water supply, and fishing and farming have suffered. Protests by villages have forced both the electricity company and the authorities in Brazil to take action – they have reduced pollution, provided materials to build wells and taken steps to control malaria. But the River Uatuma is dead and this is not enough for the protestors. The Balbina Project has meant the hazards of dam building have become the subject of national public debate.

Agriculture and change

▶ **How is the land made productive?**
▶ **What are the different types of agriculture?**

Farms for wealth

Since Europeans colonized Brazil in the sixteenth century farming has dramatically changed the landscape.

Now Brazil is one of the three largest producers in the world of soybean, maize, cocoa, coffee, oranges, sugar cane, cassava, banana, cashew nuts, pepper, beef, chicken and castor seed. It is amongst the ten largest producers of tobacco, pork, jute, cotton, eggs, honey, peanuts, rice and milk. These are important for export, as well as providing for home needs.

Fruits, vegetables and soybean are recent additions to the list of exports. Since 1975 soybean has been adapted to the central **savannas** (*cerrados*) of Brazil. Over 50 per cent of Brazil's greatly increased production now comes from this area.

Each type of farming is dominant in different regions (map **A**), and each system creates its own particular landscape (photos **B** and **C**).

B Cocoa plantation in Bahia

A Farming regions in Brazil

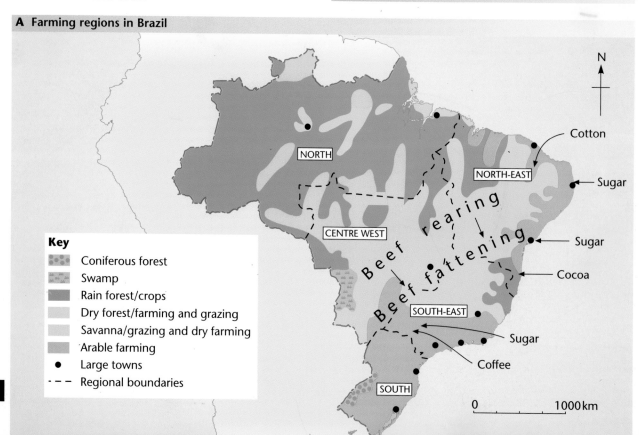

Key
- Coniferous forest
- Swamp
- Rain forest/crops
- Dry forest/farming and grazing
- Savanna/grazing and dry farming
- Arable farming
- ● Large towns
- - - - Regional boundaries

N

Cotton
Sugar
Cocoa
Sugar
Coffee
Sugar

Beef rearing
Beef fattening

NORTH
NORTH-EAST
CENTRE WEST
SOUTH-EAST
SOUTH

0   1000 km

32

C Smallholding men at work harvesting maize in Vitoria, Paraná

Farming to eat

Beans and maize are grown nearly everywhere (and wheat in the south) and are a part of people's staple diet (photo C). Beef cattle, sheep, goats and pigs are reared in great numbers. Large ranches have been created on the savanna lands of the Mato Grosso and by deforestation in eastern Amazonia. Cattle are reared on the less productive land and fattened up nearer to the east coast (map A).

Land divisions

Some farms in Brazil are huge. In the Centre West Region, where there are many cattle ranches, the average size is 350 hectares. In other regions the average varies between 50 and 100 hectares.

These averages disguise the differences between the few giant commercial plantations and ranches which can be several thousand hectares, and the peasant smallholdings of just a few hectares each.

Some large farms are the result of land taken in colonial times (*latifundios*), and some were more recently bought on the **pioneer fringe**. Many *latifundios* are subdivided and let out to peasants for rent or a share of their crop. In fact smallholdings are often more productive than large farms. In north-east Brazil farms over 500 hectares in area produce on average $2 per hectare. Farms up to ten hectares in size produce $85 per hectare.

Land ownership is a real issue in Brazil (see pages 50–1). Although 4.5 million people own farms, 5 per cent of the owners have 65 per cent of the land. Some twelve million rural people are landless peasants.

FACT FILE

Agro-ecology
Brazilian agriculturist Marc von der Weid explains:

'Brazil's future agricultural development should look for ways to obtain maximum yield at minimal risk. This means understanding the ways in which agriculture works in an **ecosystem** (agro-ecology). This kind of approach is quite different to the approach common at the moment, which relies on the use of chemicals to change the ecosystem.

Organic agricultural researchers working with small farmers in Brazil have doubled and tripled yields for beans and maize. The approach involved the selection and breeding of local varieties, use of green organic manure, crop rotation and methods to control soil erosion, all along with pest control and agro-forestry.'

Managing agricultural development in Amazonia

▶ What are the alternative types of farming?

Traditional farming, agro-forestry, ranching and small-scale crop farming are all examples of agricultural development in Amazonia.

Traditional farming

Agro-forestry

Agro-forestry is a combination of forestry, tree crops and arable farming. Japanese settlers have practised agro-forestry at Tomé-Açu, 115 kilometres south of Belém, since 1929. In the 1950s there was a boom in black pepper, their main crop. But a drop in world prices and an attack of fungus brought the boom to an end, and the farmers moved onto a mixture of crops.

A Traditional farming in Amazonia – a method used by indigenous people for a thousand years

Features of the *selvas*
- Very thick high forest
- Thick undergrowth and many weeds near rivers
- Thin soils easily washed away
- Most minerals and plant foods are held in the trees and undergrowth, not in the soil
- Very heavy rainstorms
- Strong sun between rains
- Many plant diseases and insects
- No real winter, and in many places no dry season

Features of shifting cultivation: 'slash and burn'
- A small plot is chosen to be cleared for farming.
- Most trees are cut down, but not uprooted.
- Some trees are left, spaced out at intervals.
- Undergrowth is cut.
- The plot is burned over for several days, leaving lots of ashes. Crops are planted as soon as the burning has finished.
- A mixture of crops is grown – sweet potato, manioc, fruit, maize, vegetables – all mixed in amongst one another.
- After two or three years of crops the plot is abandoned.
- A new plot is cleared each year to keep the rotation going. A farmer has several plots planted each year. He may come back to a plot and clear it again after about ten years.

Dangers for the crop farmer
- Most minerals and plant foods may be lost when the trees and undergrowth are destroyed.
- The sun and rain will make the soil very infertile after a couple of years.
- The thin layer of soil can be washed away by heavy rain.
- The sun burns up young plants.
- Weeds, plant diseases and insects may still be in the soil.

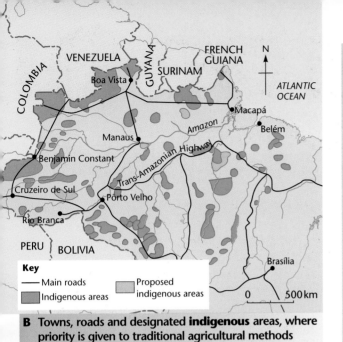

B Towns, roads and designated **indigenous** areas, where priority is given to traditional agricultural methods

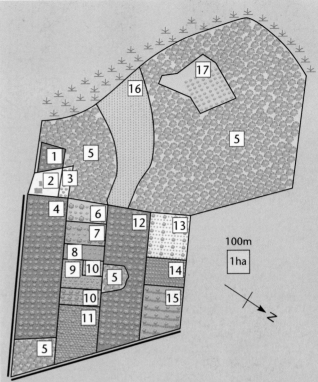

Key

1	Cocoa	8	Rubber trees
2	Household area	9	Rubber trees, black pepper, cocoa
3	Coconut, citrus, mangosteen, graviola	10	Rubber trees, passion fruit
4	Cocoa, erythrina, andiroba, Brazil nut	11	Black pepper
5	Secondary forest regeneration	12	Cocoa, banana
		13	Black pepper, cupuacu
6	Cocoa, vanilla, palheteira, freijo	14	Black pepper
		15	Passion fruit, cupuacu
7	Cocoa, parica	16	Pasture grasses
		17	Black pepper, clearing

Mangosteen, graviola, cupuacu – fruit trees
Erythrina, palheteira, freijo, parica – trees grown for shade
Andiroba – oil seed tree

C Land use on a Japanese farm in Tomé-Açu

There are now 280 farms around Tomé-Açu, averaging 150 hectares. Each farm grows crops on about 20 hectares; the rest is rotated for forest and tree crops (map **C**). Over 55 different crops are grown, as well as tree crops and vegetables.

Ranching

Ranchers have been working their way west extending the traditional cattle lands of the north-west and Mato Grosso Plateau. Huge areas of land are bought. The forest is cleared by burning and using earth moving equipment.

Now there are more than 50 000 livestock farms in Amazonia. Although each hectare produces little, large areas can mean good profits. It is not certain what this kind of farming will do to the soil and whether the pastures will survive.

Cattle occupy large areas of land with little labour, and timber and minerals can bring extra profits. Rich families, Brazilian companies and transnational companies have invested in land in Brazil, helped by government **subsidies** and tax breaks.

Small-scale crop farming

Since 1972 Brazilians have been able to get land grants of 100 hectares near to the new highways through Amazonia. Most farmers struggled for many years as they gradually cleared their plot and learned how to survive the equatorial conditions. Many with plots on poor soils or with land that frequently flooded had to give up and sell to ranchers. Others made good.

FACT FILE

Antonio and Jovante – small-scale farmers
In 1972 Antonio and Jovante and their three small children took a 100 hectare plot on the side of the Trans-Amazonian Highway. They managed to build their own house and survive floods flowing off the road. They grew mainly rice, but production was low and clearing the land was slow. During the first seven years the family often had to go back to stay with relatives because of illness or a shortage of food, and leave Antonio to farm alone. They used all their savings, but survived and now make a living with their rice sales.

Roraima – regional development in part of Amazonia

▶ Where will this development lead?

Roraima State

Roraima is a state in the north of the Amazon Basin. It is home for several thousand **indigenous** people – **savanna** Indians like the Makuxi and the Wapixana, and forest Indians like the Yanomami. Agriculture and settlement are developing fast and now over 300 000 people live in Roraima (table **E**). It is nearly twice the size of England, where 50 million people live.

Boa Vista is the main town (photo **A**). You can see that space is not a main concern in town planning.

Roraima has a real dry season (graph **C**) unlike much of Amazonia, and in the north especially there are grasslands or savanna (map **B**). In the 1970s grain production was encouraged by land grants. In the south of the state owners made improvements to their estates. Then the BR174 road was completed linking Roraima with Manaus.

Rural development since 1980

Cattle are a main source of wealth, and 75 per cent of bank grants have been for livestock developments. Now there are more than 7000 farms rearing over 400 000 cattle, many on pastures planted after clearing forest.

Many estates have a mixture of crops and animals, and several thousand farms are purely arable. The main crops are rice (grown on the river flood plains – the *Varzea*), maize, beans and manioc. These crops are often grown in sequence as a rotation. Banana trees are also important.

Gold

In 1987–90 there was a gold-rush to the Yanomami Indians' lands in the north-west of the state. Prospectors (called *garimpeiros*) came from all over Brazil. Almost every family in Roraima sent someone to the gold fields, so arable production went down while the gold-rush lasted.

Now only a few miners make a living from the gold, but in 1990 there were still some 40 000 poor and desperate *garimpeiros* on Yanomami land. They killed many of the animals the Indians relied on for food.

A Aerial view of Boa Vista

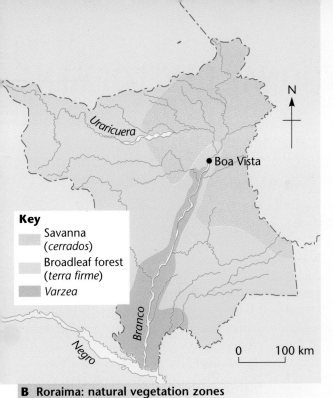

Key

	Savanna (*cerrados*)
	Broadleaf forest (*terra firme*)
	Varzea

B Roraima: natural vegetation zones

Recent trends

Areas are being colonized around the settlements (map **D**) and forest cleared. Mixed farming is being encouraged, especially rice, the staple food. In 1981 there were 500 hectares of rice farming; now there are well over 7000 hectares on the *Varzea* along the River Branco and River Uraricuera. Large estates are common, with 70 per cent of farms being over 1000 hectares.

Like the rest of Brazil, Roraima has its problems of inequality, with squatters and small farmers struggling for justice. This, along with illness and poor transport in the wet season, are major issues for Roraima.

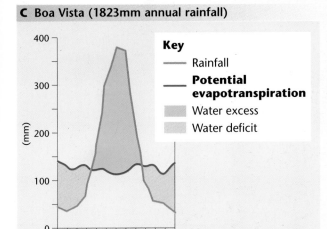

C Boa Vista (1823mm annual rainfall)

Key
- Rainfall
- **Potential evapotranspiration**
- Water excess
- Water deficit

D Roraima: settlement, main roads and colonization

Key
- Colonization areas
- Settlements

	Population in thousands				
	1950	**1960**	**1970**	**1980**	**1990**
Roraima State	19	25	43	75	275
Boa Vista town	5	10	15	29	150

E Roraima and Boa Vista: population growth (BR174 opened in 1978)

FACT FILE

Population density

As well as in Roraima, the population has also been increasing in other parts of Amazonia, as the following table shows:

	1980	1988
Brazil	14.07	17.63
North Region	1.65	2.58
Roraima State	0.34	0.57
Rondonia State	2.02	4.28
Acre State	1.97	2.68
Amazonas State	0.92	1.37
Para State	2.77	4.01
Amapa State	1.26	1.67
Tocantins State	no data	3.84

Changes in population density, people per square kilometre

37

Economic change

▶ How is Brazil's economy changing?

Brazil has changed dramatically in the last 25 years. Alongside Mexico it qualifies as a Latin American **newly industrialized country**. It is waiting in the wings with China and India to be part of the powerful and rich core of a new world order.

In the past the USA has dominated Latin America. The US Secret Service (the CIA) and US companies (**TNCs**) have influenced politics and economic growth. Now countries like Brazil and Mexico are challenging this situation.

Population and wealth
Brazil's population is still increasing fast but the economy is keeping pace. Brazil is now the tenth largest economy in the world, and much of this wealth is created by services and industry (tables **A** and **B**). But in spite of this Brazil has many millions of people in **absolute poverty**.

	1960	1993
Population (millions)	72.6	156.5
Real GDP (US$)	1404	5500
Infant mortality rate (deaths under one year old per 1000 live births)	116	57

A Growth in population and national wealth

	% GDP	% workforce
Agriculture	10	23
Industry	38	24
Services	52	53

B The structure of the economy, 1994

Expansion and change
The frontier of agricultural settlement is being rapidly pushed back. The area of rural estates in Brazil increased from 293 million hectares in 1970 to 376 million hectares in 1985, an addition of about six times the area of England! Agricultural production is also increasing, and from 1982 to 1990 output grew by 38 per cent. Much of the increase is due to more intensive use of existing farmland, for example by using new seeds, fertilizers, pesticides and irrigation.

At the same time the structure of the economy as a whole is changing, especially the balance between primary production, industry and services (graph C).

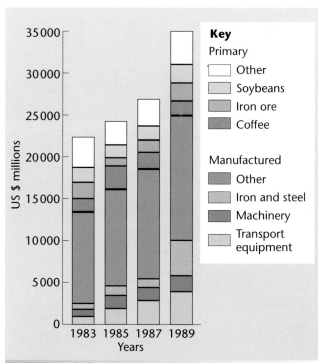

C Structural change: composition of exports, 1983–9

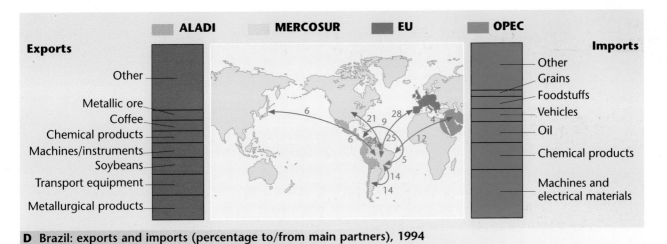

ALADI   **MERCOSUR**   **EU**   **OPEC**

Exports

- Other
- Metallic ore
- Coffee
- Chemical products
- Machines/instruments
- Soybeans
- Transport equipment
- Metallurgical products

Imports

- Other
- Grains
- Foodstuffs
- Vehicles
- Oil
- Chemical products
- Machines and electrical materials

D Brazil: exports and imports (percentage to/from main partners), 1994

The informal economy

Alongside the official economy is a flourishing informal economy – people working without official records. Forty per cent of the working population is involved. These people, who may work as street sellers, repairers or decorators, work full time or just a few hours a week. Many work in the workshops and cafés which are found everywhere in the *favelas* and poorer areas. Without the informal economy many more millions would be without income.

International finance

In the 1970s a global economic boom and very high prices for oil produced a lot of spare **capital** in the banks of the world. As a result large amounts were lent to developing countries. Brazil borrowed vast amounts from the World Bank and private banks in Europe, Japan and the USA. By 1986 Brazil's debt was US $112 billion. Brazil uses up most of its trading profits just to pay the interest on these loans.

The international banks and the **IMF** (International Monetary Fund) have put pressure on Brazil to make changes to the economy. Brazil has had to open up trade, reduce government spending and reduce the value of the currency – a Structural Adjustment Policy (SAP).

These measures attract foreign investment, reduce **inflation** and make the economy more stable, but increase the prices in the shops and reduce public services like health, education and benefits. Generally the poor suffer while business improves (cartoon **E**).

FACT FILE

A long way to go . . .
Brazil, under a military dictatorship for much of the time, has had some success in striving to become a global power, but is still a long way from a stable economic system.

Not only are there stark regional differences in wealth in Brazil, with the North-East Region, an area of desperate poverty, but the unequal distribution of wealth also leaves the poor everywhere struggling.

For example, in Mato Grosso State the health of the poor in small towns is imperilled because they cannot afford medicines even if they gain access to a doctor. In Cuiaba City, 20 per cent of the children suffer from malnutrition. From a population of some 60 families, in the small town of Nova Alvorada, only fifteen women can read at even the most basic level.

E The results of the structural adjustment policy

National development issues

There are plenty of issues in every nation, and Brazil is no exception. They are environmental, economic, social and political, but one theme runs through them all – justice. There are strong forces working for justice in Brazil, in particular the Catholic Church which champions the cause of the poor and oppressed.

Justice for the poor

Brazil has been called 'a rich country of poor people'. It is estimated that in 1990, 55 per cent of urban households and 87 per cent of rural households were living in poverty.

The rural poor are often even worse off than the urban poor, but are hidden away from public view in the remote countryside. Many landless peasants are working for very low wages with no job security. Farmers with very small plots of rented land pay as much as half of their production to the landowner.

Justice for the young

The plight of some children in the cities, especially street children, is described on pages 26–7. Many children do not get the chance to go to school; many are used as child labour in unsuitable conditions.

Justice for women

Discrimination against women is common, as it is in most countries of the world. Women's wages are generally lower than men's, and they are expected to take on whatever work is available. Many suffer hardship and poverty.

Justice on the land

The problems of land ownership and squatting in rural areas are very difficult to deal with. Landless people feel they are entitled to occupy unused land. Small farmers are often in danger of being forced off their land. But large landowners feel they need protection against illegal squatters.

Political justice

Brazil is a young democracy and from time to time the military have taken over and imposed a dictatorship. Often government has been unstable and bribery and corruption have been a problem.

Justice in the economy

Brazil has seen rapid growth in production and in exports. At the same time international debt has grown and public spending increased. In Brazil this led to rapid **inflation** – sometimes at the end of a year money was worth less than half its value at the beginning of the year. So each year wages had to go up for people to survive, and savings could disappear.

In the early 1990s the inflation rate was 300 per cent per annum. Hyperinflation like this affects everyone, but the problem is how to control it without making life even harder for the poor.

Racial justice

Prejudice and discrimination against black and mixed race people in Brazil are widespread. They suffer particularly from poverty, unemployment and ill health.

Global justice

It can be argued that people in Brazil have been **exploited** throughout the country's history – first throughout the colonial period by the Portuguese, then by the nations of the industrialized world taking resources and raw materials at low cost. Now Brazil looks for justice in financial dealings and trade but world trade agreements still favour the richest nations.

Natural
These are questions about the environment - energy, air, water, soil, living things and their relationships to each other. These questions are about the built as well as the 'natural' environment.

Who decides?
These are questions about power, who makes choices and decides what is to happen; who benefits and loses as a result of these decisions and at what cost.

Economic
These are questions about money, trading, aid, ownership, buying and selling.

Social
These are questions about people, their relationships, their traditions, culture and the way they live. They include questions about how, for example, gender, race, disability, class and age affect social relationships.

A Development Compass Rose

(Source: the Development Education Centre, Birmingham)

The Development Compass Rose

This compass rose is an aid to the study of development issues. It suggests you ask questions about all the dimensions of an issue:

- Natural/environmental
- Economic
- Social
- Who decides?/political.

An issue can be placed at the centre of the rose. You could start from a photograph, a map, a case study or a piece of text. The example here shows a photo from Combu Island, Amazonia. A cocoa farming family are preparing harvested cocoa beans – part of the wife and mother's 'unpaid' work. Questions can be written around the issue in each direction.

FACT FILE

Questions that can be asked about the photo:

N: What conditions are needed to grow cocoa beans?
What kind of plant do they grow on?
What materials is the house made of?

E: Will these beans be sold? Where?
How much is the woman paid?
Is the child helping?

S: What other work does the woman have?
Is this work fulfilling her potential?
Why is the man just sitting?

W: Who decides what happens?
Who takes what from the proceeds?
Is the woman in control of her work?
Who decides who should work?

▶ What are Brazil's successes?

▶ What has been the price of success?

Brazil's industries grew rapidly in the 1980s. Growth was based on cheap **labour** and a hard-working expanding population, vast natural resources and huge loans from the rich countries of the world.

An **industrial heartland** has grown up around São Paulo (photo B), and growth has continued into the 1990s (table A). This growing industrial region now covers an area 100 kilometres by 60 kilometres.

Steel production

The steel and car industries are the basis for the industrial heartland (Map C).

	1989	1994
Automobiles	731 000	1 249 000
Tractors	34 000	43 000
Electronic items	8 400 000	12 700 000
Electric items	18 000 000	22 700 000

A Brazil: industrial growth

The first **integrated steelworks** in Brazil were built at Volta Redonda in 1947. Now there are five, all in the south-east where there is iron ore, limestone, manganese, HEP (all needed for steel production) and the main concentration of workers and markets. Only the coal/coke has to be imported. In 1994 Brazil produced over 25 million tonnes of steel and was eighth in the world rankings.

Steel users

Nearby in São Paulo is most of the car industry. While the steel industry is mainly Brazilian owned, the cars are produced mostly by foreign companies: Volkswagen, Fiat, General Motors and Ford amongst others.

Other steel using industries are located in the south-east, for example Brazil is the sixth largest aircraft manufacturer in the world. Recently, with Brazil becoming a regional power, the weapons industry has also grown.

B Industrial estate in São Paulo

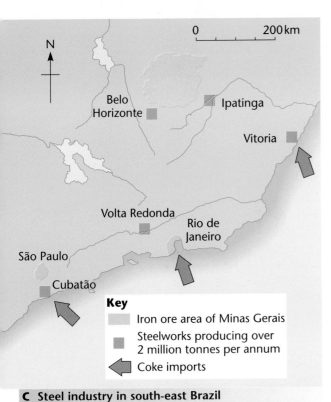

C Steel industry in south-east Brazil

Key
- Iron ore area of Minas Gerais
- Steelworks producing over 2 million tonnes per annum
- Coke imports

D The darker side of economic success

There are over 2000 foreign companies in São Paulo alone, many associated with the steel and car industries.

The darker side

The increased national income from industrial development means greater wealth for the government, for management and for owners and investors. When the income is justly divided it can mean greater wealth for the population in general. But when unemployment is above 30 per cent, life can be difficult for the work-force (box **E**).

E FROM THE SHOP FLOOR

'The main problem today is pay and fatigue because of compulsory overtime. The workers have to achieve production targets set by management and this means twelve-hour shifts. Workers do it for a week, or two weeks, but can't manage it for more. It is illegal to do more than two hours overtime, and it is illegal for women to do any overtime. But women are doing twelve-hour shifts.'

Unilever worker, interview with Brazil Network, 1989

'Working conditions are terrible. They really exploit us. We have to work on Saturdays and a 47-hour week. As most of the employees are women, most of the spare time is spent doing housework. The speed at which we are forced to work has been increasing. One person often does the work that used to be done by three. As well as being tiring this speed-up has caused a lot of tenseness and illness, especially problems with nerves and headaches to go with the backaches we've always had. In many parts of the factories the noise, dust and heat cause health problems.'

Letter to Network Brazil in 1988 from workers at Linhas Correntes, São Paulo, subsidiary of Coats Viyella, UK

FACT FILE

The steel industry is one of the foundations of Brazil's economic growth. The table shows how it compares to the rest of the world.

Steel production: a time of change, 1967–80 in rank order

	1980 output (million tonnes)	% change 1967–80		1980 output (million tonnes)	% change 1967–80
Japan	112	+64	Brazil	17	+331
USA	112	−12	Spain	14	+179
West Germany	48	+19	UK	12	−54
Italy	29	+67	India	12	+61
France	26	+18	South Korea	12	+3514
Belgium	19	+19	Australia	8	+151
Canada	18	+81			

The weapons industry

▶ How does a weapons industry fit into national development?

National defence

Over the last twenty years Brazil has developed a major weapons industry (photo **A**). This was encouraged partly because the USA stopped selling arms to Brazil during the Vietnam War, which ended in 1975. Brazil also has a very powerful military, who felt the country could not afford to rely on foreign weapons.

Brazil has defence commitments on its borders (map **B**). It fears interference from other countries since the Falklands (Malvinas) War between Argentina and the UK, and has problems from drug traffickers and guerrillas along its borders. The military also have to deal with illegal gold miners in Amazonia, and monitor the policy of Indian integration.

A Tucano training aircraft, bought by the RAF and assembled in Belfast from parts made in Brazil

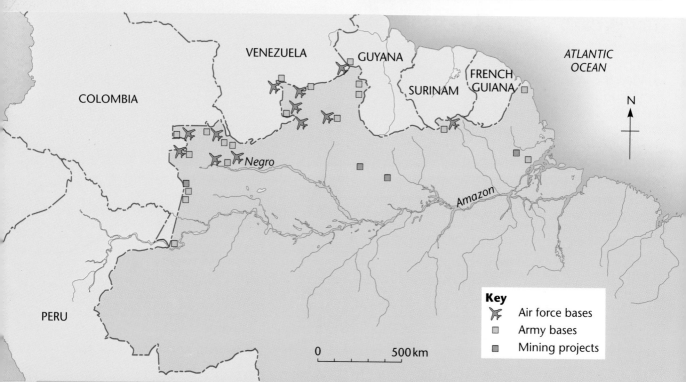

Key

✈ Air force bases

▫ Army bases

▪ Mining projects

0 ____ 500 km

B Army and air force bases along Brazil's northern frontier, in the Calha Norte Project area (an important government development scheme)

Location of the weapons industry

The government produced a strategic plan to develop a weapons industry focused along the South Paraíba (*Paraíba do Sul*) Valley (map **C**). The valley is close to both the military decision making centres at Rio and the industrial core of the nation around São Paulo. It is also the main route into the Brazilian Plateau, and on into Amazonia.

Eighty per cent of the weapons industries are in this valley. AVIBRAS the main missile manufacturer, ENGESA the specialized engineers and CTA the air force technology centre have all been sited here. Nuclear research and development centres are in São Paulo and St. José dos Campos.

Brazil has fewer people in its armed forces for the size of its population than the UK (table **D**), but it has a very large Public Security Force under army control.

Brazil is now an exporter of weapons, but still small by comparison with even the UK, let alone the USA.

	Brazil	UK	USA
GDP (US$ billions)	459	1104	5522
Defence budget (US$ billions)	7	34	278
Armed forces (000s)	295	240	1547
Public Security Forces (000s)	385	n/a	n/a
Population (millions)	163	57	249

D Military forces, 1994

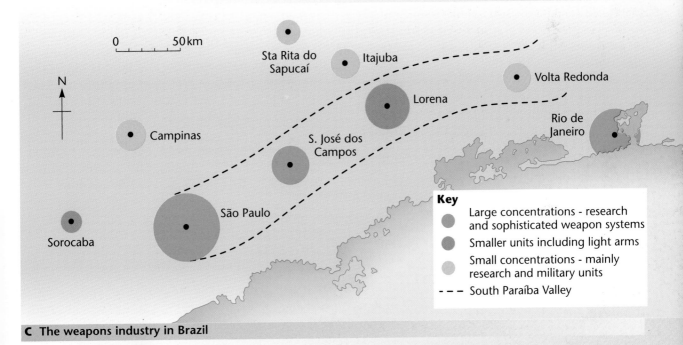

C The weapons industry in Brazil

Key
- Large concentrations - research and sophisticated weapon systems
- Smaller units including light arms
- Small concentrations - mainly research and military units
- --- South Paraíba Valley

FACT FILE

Military expenditure and alternatives
Annual world military expenditure: US $1 000 000 million

What (in US $ million) it would require worldwide to:			
• provide clean water	50 000m	• prevent global warming	8000m
• provide safe energy	50 000m	• prevent acid rain	8000m
• end Third World debts	30 000m	• stop deforestation	7000m
• prevent soil erosion	24 000m	• stop loss of ozone	5000m
• provide shelter	21 000m	• eliminate illiteracy	5000m
• eliminate malnutrition	15 000m		

Total expenditure for the whole world: **US $223 000 million**

(Source: Colm Regan (ed), 75/25, DEC(Bhm) (1996) p.202, fig. 14.2)

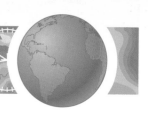

Resources and power

▶ How do natural resources influence Brazil's development?

Massive resources

Brazil has huge mineral and energy resources (map **A**), many still untapped in the Amazon Basin. The Grand Carajás programme (pages 58–9) provides an example of large-scale mining in Brazil.

Some oil wells are developed, especially off-shore along the east coast, and in 1995 Brazil produced half its oil and gas needs. There are four oil refineries in the **industrial heartland** around São Paulo. But Brazil is still relatively short of oil.

To overcome its shortage of oil Brazil turns sugar cane, produced on massive sugar cane estates, into alcohol. More than half of Brazil's cars run on a mixture of petrol and alcohol.

Brazil has to rely heavily on hydroelectricity for energy, supplemented by imported coal and oil (table **B**).

Source	1979 %	1994 %	Source	1979 %	1994 %
Hydroelectricity	25	38	Natural gas	1	2
Wood	22	13	Coal	4	5
Sugar cane	6	10	Nuclear	0	0.1
Oil	41	31	Others	1	0.9

B Energy sources in Brazil (in percentages)

Hydroelectric power

The Brazilian government has planned very large HEP schemes, with high dams creating huge reservoirs. Those in the Amazon Basin flood large areas, because the land is flat and the gradient of the river valleys gentle. Pages 30–1 discussed some of the issues surrounding large HEP schemes.

Map **C** shows the area with the greatest number of developed HEP schemes, on the Paraná and its tributaries. The world's largest HEP plant at Itaipu (photo **D**) generates 12.6 million kilowatts of electricity, which would be enough for one-fifth of UK requirements. It is a joint project between Brazil and Paraguay, with the power divided equally between the two countries.

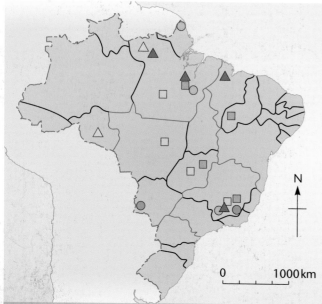

Key
△ Tin (2nd)
○ Iron ore (3rd)
● Manganese (4th)
▲ Aluminium (6th)
■ Nickel (7th)
□ Gold (7th)

N

0   1000 km

(Position in world production is shown in the key.) Besides these major minerals Brazil also mines: lead, copper, niobium, titanium, tungsten, zinc, amianthus, limestone, diamonds, phosphates, quartz, salt, coal, oil, thorium and uranium.

A Some of Brazil's mineral resources

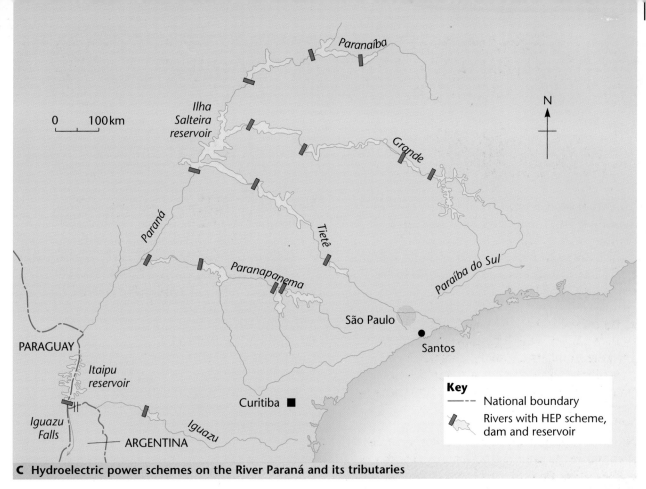

C Hydroelectric power schemes on the River Paraná and its tributaries

Key
- - - - National boundary
Rivers with HEP scheme, dam and reservoir

FACT FILE
Mineral and energy reserves

	Location	Million tonnes
Gypsum	Altamira	1000
	Itaituba	1300
Bauxite	Xingu–Manaus	4000
	Paragominas	1000
Kaolin	Rio Negro	500
	Rio Jari	365
Iron	Amapá	100
	Carajás	19 000
	Xingu	100
Manganese	Amapá	50
	Carajás	60
Copper	Carajás	1000
Nickel	Carajás	120
Diamonds	Marabá	?
Zinc	Rondônia	0.1
Natural Gas	Jurua	1300
	Amapá	13 000
Petroleum	Acre	6000

D Itaipu Dam on the River Paraná

47

Agribusiness in the São Francisco Valley

▶ **How do the large companies and local people benefit from agribusiness?**

Agribusiness is booming around the world, including in Brazil where multinational companies are encouraged to invest. Agribusiness usually involves modern farming techniques, such as high yield varieties of seeds, fertilizers, pest and disease control, and either mechanization or a stable cheap supply of **labour**.

Changes in the Lower São Francisco Valley

The valley between the Sobradinho and Itaparica Dams is in the drought zone of north-east Brazil (map A). It only receives between 350 and 600 millimetres of rainfall a year. Peasant farmers rented small farms from two rich families who owned most of the land. They produced beans, maize and cattle for subsistence.

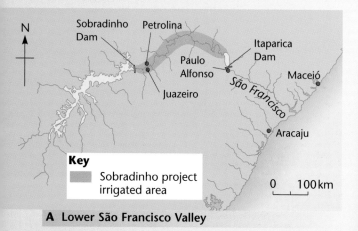

Key
Sobradinho project irrigated area

0   100km

A Lower São Francisco Valley

In 1978 when the massive Sobradinho Dam was completed, 64 000 people were moved from the area that was flooded. Most had nowhere to go and ended up in squatter settlements.

The main reason for building the dam was to produce electricity, but irrigation systems were also set up under state control. By 1990, 910 square kilometres were irrigated and the area had become an important fruit producing region (photo B).

Irrigated farms

There are eight farms of over 40 square kilometres each, 150 medium-sized farms with more than ten hectares, and over 2000 small farms in the Sobradinho scheme. Most of these are on land now owned by the state.

Much fruit is exported to Europe. The remainder is sold to supermarket chains in south central Brazil or the north-east. Other farms produce tomatoes, sugar, cotton, beans, onions and seeds. Box C lists some of the requirements for commercial fruit and vegetable farming.

Now the area has the highest use of fertilizers, tractors and irrigation in the north-east, and the highest investment and productivity. The twin cities of Petrolina and Juazeiro have doubled in size to half a million. They have industries to make juices, fertilizers and agricultural machinery.

B Fruit farming in the São Francisco Valley

C NEEDS OF FRUIT AND VEGETABLE BUSINESS

Markets to sell produce
- Access to global markets all the year round e.g. from Brazil by air (grapes) or refrigerated ship (melons, mangoes, papayas, vegetables)
- Access to markets with large demand for seasonal crops e.g. city supermarkets in Brazil

Growing conditions
- Mainly frost-free
- Reliable controlled water supply (irrigation)
- Flat or terraced land for crops
- Fertile soil (using fertilizers if necessary)

Space
- Access to farmland owned, rented or under contract
- Sites for processing plants

Labour
- Reliable skilful workers
- Large numbers in certain seasons

Capital and finance
- Capital to buy land, build plants, grow or buy crops, pay wages, transport and market produce

Reliable and helpful host government

D A SHARECROPPER'S EXPERIENCE

'We used to sharecrop a small farm, giving the landlord half of our crop as rent each year. When the dam was built our land and home were flooded.

We spent some time in a shanty town but then were lucky to be given an allotment of land from the state. We couldn't afford to put in irrigation pumps and pipes, but a Japanese firm rented the land from us, irrigated it and planted mango.

Now the Japanese employ us and we live on our land and care for the plants and build wooden crates to export the fruit. For this we get a share of the crop.'

The labour supply

Most of the crops grown in the valley are extremely labour-intensive. Much of the work is contracted out, with a certain payment for a certain task (piece-work). This means a worker will use family labour to help complete the task quickly. Though officially there is no child labour here, children are seen working in nearly every field.

Local labour recruited for most crops is mainly women. Women are preferred because they are seen as skilful and 'better workers'. But because of their responsibilities with the family and home, they take flexible part-time work. They are less likely to organize themselves into a union, so they don't receive benefits like sick pay or a pension.

Migrant labour is used mainly for harvesting tomatoes and sugar cane. Thousands of men come from the *sertao* (see page 56) of the north-east, their travel paid for by the big companies. Some work in the fields, others in the processing plants. They have little power once they arrive, and often their wage rates are changed in response to supply and demand. They live in shacks, or find rooms in local towns.

FACT FILE

Unions in Petrolina and Juazeiro
In 1994, with support from the labourers, two unions signed the first collective agreement with owners in the São Francisco Valley. The owners agreed a minimum wage (US $110 per month) and the registration of workers by employers to give them basic social rights.

Forty per cent of the families in Juazeiro live in poverty. What is this wage worth? It is just about enough to buy a basic food ration for a family. The workers 'lucky enough' to get this wage, work mainly in the vineyards, five to a hectare, doing two or three pickings of 30 tonnes each. If the owners paid them US $200 per month there would be no profit because the price of grapes is too low.

Conflict over land

Land and land ownership are a continual source of conflict in Brazil. One per cent of the landowners control over half of all the land. Huge areas, like the sugar cane estates in São Paulo State and the cattle ranches in Pará State, are owned either by large companies or by rich families. Land conflicts have captured the imagination in Brazil – every night 50 million people watch *Cattle Kings*, a television serial about farming in Amazonia.

Conflict in Pará State

The population of Pará State increased by ten times in the 1980s. One attraction was the gold-rush to Serra Pelada. Over 100 000 hopeful miners flocked to work in terrible conditions in the open-cast mine. Few made their fortune but the people are still in the area.

Many unemployed people from the North-East Region and from the *favelas* of big cities have migrated to Pará. They are partly encouraged by government laws that allow the occupation of unused land. The Land Reform Agency can confiscate any forest land, or agree to its invasion by landless people.

Macaxeiros Ranch, Pará State

Macaxeiros is near to El Dorado, once a boom town for the Serra Pelada gold-rush. Immigrant groups from *favelas* have set up camp and begun to clear and farm land on the edge of Macaxeiros Ranch. They have organized their own rules against drugs, alcohol and bad behaviour, and have set up a school.

The ranch is owned by the Ribera family with nine children, who came as pioneers. They sold everything to buy the 6000 hectares of land. They have 5000 cattle, and some of their land is still forested. The local ranch owners have formed an association to fight against the invasions of their land.

> They are bandits, murderers, bad people from the cities.

Mrs Ribera, rancher

> They are rich, liars, exploiters who don't care about people.

Landless people's school teacher

A Mutual hatred at Macaxeiros

The landless people are in the MST (*Movimiento Sem Terra* – organization of landless people), now a political party that believes in communal ownership of the land.

The conflict here is fierce. In April 1996, nineteen people were shot dead by the police during a peaceful protest blocking a main road – an event called 'The massacre of the landless'.

We are interested in working the land as a cooperative. Together we can afford to hire a tractor and buy in bulk. We will be able to borrow money and maybe get better services – electricity, water, transport.

B Verdun soon after the 1990 invasion

C Solange Czycza, landless community leader near Verdun

Verdun, Paraná State

The building of the Itaipu and Segredo Dams on the River Paraná flooded areas that displaced more than 100 000 people. Others in this part of Brazil have lost their farmwork because of mechanization. Some small landowners have lost their farms because of high interest rates.

These landless people can see land standing idle for years. Land occupied for a year can be legally claimed. Verdun (photo **B**) is one of 6000 settlements established in Brazil by landless people since 1989.

In 1988 fifty families occupied land at Verdun. They were soon evicted by police. In 1990, with a new State Governor, they tried again. The owner employed three gunmen to threaten and frighten the settlers. The landless people eventually got help from the MST and other local settlements, and forced the gunmen to leave. Each invasion of land has its own complicated story of rights and wrongs.

FACT FILE

Trouble in the State of Maranhão

Farmer Francisco Ferreira was killed in the village of Peritoro by two gunmen hired by rancher Jonas da Cruz.

This is one more death which could have been avoided if the authorities had taken seriously the complaints made since August 1989. Since then Jonas has threatened rape, expelled families, burned ten houses and blocked access roads with gunmen. The entire area, where 300 families live, is claimed by ranchers. However, it was donated to slaves in 1901 but occupied by Jonas' father in 1949 with the help of gunmen.

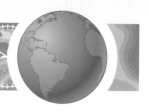

Transport development

▶ What is the importance of transport?

A country the size of Brazil needs a huge investment to maintain an efficient transport network. Years ago railways were a vital long distance link, but now the rail network is in decline and only some city commuter lines and special mining lines, as well as tram lines (photo **A**), are important. Road transport and domestic air travel have taken over.

Opening up and integrating
New roads are needed for the settlement and development of new lands. In the nineteenth and twentieth centuries the farming frontier moved inland from the east coast and road networks followed. Now the south has an efficient network stretching in towards the Paraná River (map **B**).

A Rio tram, with surfers riding on the sides

B Brazil: road network and air service

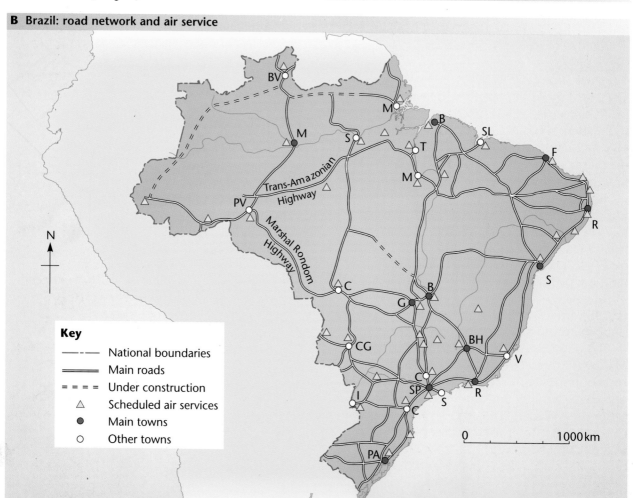

N

Trans-Amazonian Highway

Marshal Rondom Highway

Key
- – · – National boundaries
- ══ Main roads
- = = = = Under construction
- △ Scheduled air services
- ● Main towns
- ○ Other towns

0 _____ 1000 km

C Motorway to Barra da Tijuca (near Rio)

Opening up Amazonia has been made possible by building new main roads through the forests. The Trans-Amazonian Highway (map B), the first of these, was built in the 1970s, and others like the Marshal Rondom Highway, opening up Rondônia State, have followed.

Air services are very important in remote areas but only business and the richer people can afford them. The poor rely on buses for long distance travel.

On the roads

There are more and more private cars in the cities and towns, but most people still rely on taxis and buses. Local bus services are vital for urban commuters and are efficient in some cities like Curitiba (see page 55). But in the giant cities traffic generally grinds to a halt for long periods in the rush hours.

In rural areas many use local bus services to get to work each day. These are overcrowded and run down even in the richer south, and in the north and in Amazonia many local buses are ancient and unreliable. A further hazard is the mud roads in the equatorial wet season.

Motorways and new developments

Fast, efficient road transport offers new opportunities for change. Around São Paulo (map A, page 22) new motorways link the city to the surrounding area. The road through the mountains and down to the port of Santos is now a multi-lane highway. The motorway out to Campinas has encouraged the development of new industrial estates at Jundiai, 100 kilometres from São Paulo. Pepsi has sited its new massive bottling plant there.

New motorways from Rio are having similar effects. A magnificent ocean-side motorway, partly on stilts and partly through tunnels, now runs out south of Rio. Twenty kilometres on is the new town of Barra da Tijuca (photo C), with ultra-modern buildings, five kilometres of shopping malls, entertainments and space to grow.

FACT FILE

Road to destruction

The BR364 from Cuiaba to Pôrto Velho, Rondônia, was surfaced in 1981. It was part of the Polonoroeste programme made possible by loans of over $440 million from the World Bank. The project was to provide help for small farmers, improve services for new towns and protect the forest and its Indian people.

Unfortunately only the road was built. The forest, made accessible to heavy machinery, was now available to anyone, and a zone several kilometres wide each side of the road was deforested – in seven years 14 per cent of Rondônia was deforested.

The South Region

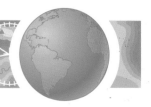

▶ How is the South Region different from the rest of Brazil?

The South Region is made up of the states of Rio Grande do Sul, Santa Catarina and Paraná. It is the most **temperate** part of Brazil and the land is very productive. It has attracted settlers from Europe in large numbers and is mainly well populated. Many settlers from Germany and Italy have stayed together to form communities where they preserve their language and culture (map **A**).

Aspects of the south have already been studied in this book, for example the climate, vegetation and farming, the HEP schemes, the conflict over land, the movement of people into and out of the region. Many small farmers suffer from lack of funds and competition from larger enterprises. However, the region has its successes too, for example the tourist park at the Iguazu Falls and Curitiba – the 'green' city of Brazil.

The Iguazu/Itaipu micro-region

This **micro-region** is very attractive to tourists (map **B**). On the borders with Paraguay and Argentina, it includes the largest HEP scheme in the world (Itaipu) and the scenic wonder of an amphitheatre with 250 waterfalls (Iguazu

Falls). The town of Foz do Iguazu has increased in size to over 200 000 people from just 35 000 in 1975, and industries like cement and metals as well as services have grown up. The same pattern is seen on the Argentinian and Paraguayan sides of the border.

B The micro-region of Iguazu/Itaipu

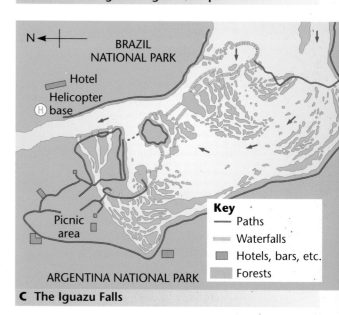

C The Iguazu Falls

A South Brazil

The actual site of the falls is being managed as a tourist park (map C), with co-operation between Brazil and Argentina. Most tourists arrive by air.

Curitiba – urban planning

Curitiba, with a population of over two million, is the 'green' city of Brazil. It shows what can be done with enthusiasm and determination by local government and people (map D and photo E).

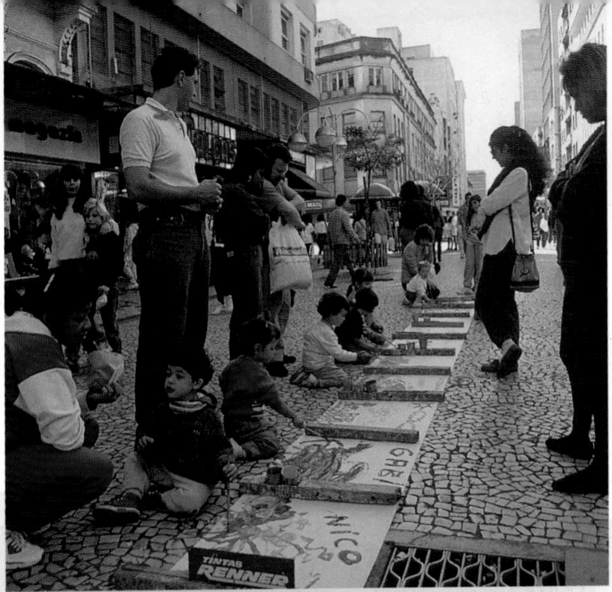

D 'Green' Curitiba

E Main **boulevard** of Curitiba, pedestrianized and site of a weekly celebration of children gathering to paint

Garbage and recycling
Residents of shanty towns which collections cannot reach are offered food and bus tokens in exchange for waste. Some 40 000 people take part in the scheme and the shanty towns are cleared up.

Planning controls
New developments must prove that they are environmentally acceptable.

City centre
The old centre has been protected by planning restrictions. New 24-hour covered street shopping arcades have been built to stop the centre becoming a 'ghost' town at night.

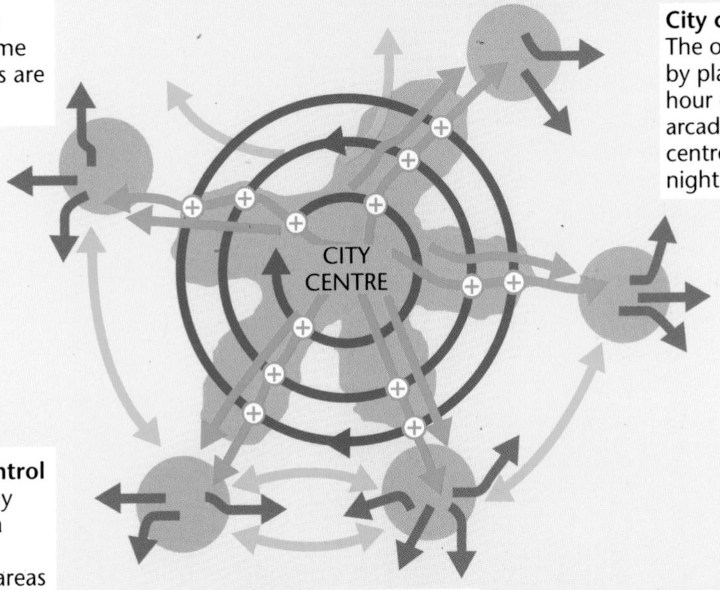

CITY CENTRE

Bus routes in the transit system

⊕ Express routes and express bus stations
— Direct routes
— Feeder routes
— Workers' routes
— Inter-district routes

Curitiba has an excellent integrated public transport system based on modern frequent buses linking the city centre and all parts of the town.

Parks and flood control
Floods and unhealthy swampy land were a major problem for Curitiba. Low-lying areas have been converted into lakeside parks and floods controlled.

Cyclists
The city has an excellent cycle path network.

The North-East Region

▶ **Can the North-East Region overcome drought, poverty and inequality?**

The North-East Region is made up of three large states (Maranhão, Paiuí and Bahia) and six smaller states. There are several different geographical regions within the political North-East Region (map **A**).

Sub-regions

Zona da Mata   Large sugar cane estates developed (box **B**) in this coastal strip behind Recife. Now diversified commercial farming is common. Soybean is grown, and the Agreste area supplies food, especially beans and maize, to the cities. People in this prosperous farming area still suffer poverty. The rural poor are often forced from the land, and many slums and shanties exist around the cities.

The south (mainly Bahia State)   Around Salvador is an exciting area, with a great variety of cultures. Its farming includes large cocoa estates. There are few droughts in the area.

The west (mainly Maranhão State)   This area is out of the drought zone and conditions are more like those of the Amazon Basin. Cattle ranching and small-scale farming are well-developed.

The *sertao*   This is a drought zone, and one of the toughest and most poverty stricken areas in Brazil. The Lower São Francisco shows how large-scale projects can change things (see pages 48–9).

Baixo Açu, Rio Grande do Norte State

The Baixo Açu river valley is in the *sertao* and liable to severe droughts. There are many small government funded dams and irrigation schemes. Most of the 17 000 new reservoirs are on private land, and 80 per cent of the water is used on larger mechanized farms. So far the major problems of the *sertao* – rural unemployment, poverty and migration – do not seem to have been helped by most of the projects.

In 1983 the Armando Ribeiro Gonçalves Dam was completed (map **C**). Box **D** suggests strategies for improvements with and without irrigation.

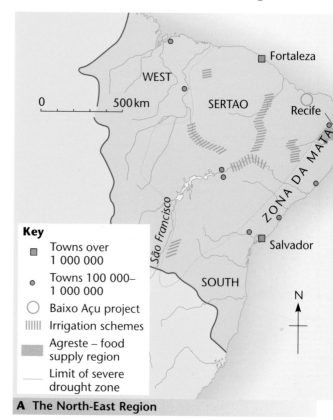

Key

▪	Towns over 1 000 000
•	Towns 100 000– 1 000 000
○	Baixo Açu project
‖‖‖	Irrigation schemes
▒	Agreste – food supply region
—	Limit of severe drought zone

A The North-East Region

B PAULO, PLANTATION OWNER

Paulo's ancestors claimed 200 hectares of land in the Zona da Mata in 1580. Now he owns 10 000 hectares and grows sugar cane and soybean. Profits from both are high. His farming is fully mechanized and relies on new seeds, fertilizer and pesticides. To increase the size of his farm he had to evict **sharecroppers** and buy up land from small farmers who couldn't compete. After disputes with peasant farmers and unions he now employs armed guards to protect his land and family.

Before
- Frequent crop failure and poor harvests due to drought.

Key
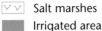
- ═══ Paved roads
- ─── Unpaved roads
- ⌄⌄ Salt marshes
- ▓ Irrigated area

Before and after
- Beans, maize and cotton trees on smallholdings.
- Competing economic activities – cattle breeding, fruit farming, textile manufacture.
- Shortage of borrowing facilities for small farmers.
- Thorny scrub on unfarmed land (*caatinga*).
- The traditional linear strips remain, farmed mainly in traditional ways (photo **E**).

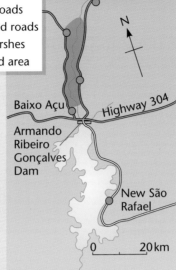

Macau

N

Baixo Açu

Highway 304

Armando Ribeiro Gonçalves Dam

New São Rafael

0   20 km

After
- 270 families relocated to New São Rafael.
- 10 000 ha irrigated.
- No water distribution system built.
- Brazilian, Japanese and American fruit corporations arrive, grow grapes and melons.
- Fruit companies buy mainly unfarmed land.
- Government promises irrigation kits (pump, hoses and money for digging canals) for small farmers, but very few arrive.
- Small farmers irrigate by hand.
- Large farms use pumping stations, concrete canals, hoses and drip feed to irrigate.

C Baixo Açu project

D STRATEGIES FOR IMPROVEMENT FOR SMALL FARMERS

- Join family plots together into a cooperative organization.
- Grow a variety of different crops.
- Look after the most vulnerable farmers with loans and help.
- Grow surplus food to eat in bad years.
- Modernize farming techniques to increase production.
- Sort out who owns the land and who can farm it.

FACT FILE

Infant deaths in a small town in the Zona da Mata

The figures in the table show the extreme poverty which exists beside great prosperity in the Zona da Mata. In 1987, there were 722 births; 322 infants died before the age of five years.

Diarrhoea	28%
Infectious childhood diseases (e.g. measles)	16%
Doomed child syndrome	15%
Weakness and wasting	15%
Fright and shock	6%
Malignant teething	5%
Diseases of skin, liver and blood	5%
Sudden death	4%
Other causes	6%

Causes of 255 deaths in the poorest families

E Traditional farming methods – donkeys used to transport water

Grand Carajás programme

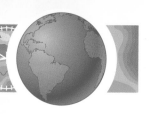

▶ How does a modern mining project operate in Amazonia?

Grand Carajás is in Pará State, part of the Amazon Basin in the North Region of Brazil. The programme is run by the Brazilian government. It includes ranching, forestry and settlement projects, but at its heart is the huge iron ore open-cast mine on Serra do Carajás (photo **B**). A new railway takes twelve trains a day (each two kilometres long!) to export 8 per cent of the world's iron ore through the port of São Luís (map **A**).

As well as iron ore, copper, manganese, nickel and bauxite are mined by a Brazilian state-owned company – Companhia do Vale do Rio Doce (CVRD). CVRD has expanded so much it is now a multinational enterprise. The **EU** has loaned US $600 million to CVRD in return for 50 per cent of the iron at a guaranteed low price. The USA has loaned a further US $300 million. The CVRD has invested US $62 000 million, which includes US $70 million on environmental projects and **indigenous** people.

'Citadel' Carajás
The CVRD has created '**citadel**' Carajás (map C) within which only permitted companies can operate. Only the 10 000 people employed directly by the company and their immediate families can live inside. The **company town** (photo **D**) has excellent facilities and very good living conditions. Around the mine deforestation has been controlled and conservation is important.

Outside the citadel there is a large Indian reserve, and colonization programmes for more than 100 square kilometres of forest. Beyond these areas ranchers, squatters and prospectors are all claiming land.

A Grand Carajás programme and surrounding area

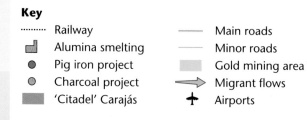

Key
.... Railway
⌐┘ Alumina smelting
● Pig iron project
○ Charcoal project
▬ 'Citadel' Carajás
— Main roads
— Minor roads
▭ Gold mining area
⇨ Migrant flows
✈ Airports

B Carajás iron ore mine

N

Belém
São Luís
Altamira
Tucuruí
Marabá
Carajás
Parauapebas
Eldorado
Corionópolis
São Félix
Xingu

0   200 km

Railway
Nine pig iron plants run on charcoal alongside railway, needing 1.5 million hectares of forest for fuel.

Marabá
Over 100 000 people. Regional highway and air traffic hub. Power substation for Tucurui electricity. Twenty iron ore smelters planned, to run on charcoal from local forests.

Tocantins

Serra Pelada
Gold mines. 100 000 miners in 1983, 30 000 in 1988. Ramshackle mining camp. Some moved on to nearby Cotia, many roam the region in search of gold.

N

Corionópolis
Early 1980s settlement, providing supplies, entertainment, prostitution.

El Dorado
See page 50.

Indian reserve
Home of 300 Xikrin Indians. Entire reserve is subject to claims by subsidiaries of CVRD. Gold panners are already polluting the rivers.

Parauapebas
Settlement at the heavily guarded entrance to citadel Carajás – provides short-term contract labour to the mines.

Colonization programme
Settlements and land organized by the government to colonize this area.

0   25km

'Citadel' Carajás
The CVRD mining area.

C Grand Carajás programme

FACT FILE

Mineral reserves

Mineral reserves in the Grand Carajás programme area

	Million tonnes
Iron	19 000
Copper	1 000
Manganese	60
Nickel	120

Also in the area are valuable reserves of bauxite, gold, tin, lead, zinc and wolfram.

No doubt other similar mining developments will take place in Amazonia. Even when a 'citadel' is set up, new industry still has a great effect on the surrounding area. Indigenous people are dispossessed of land and thousands of new migrants are attracted. Nearby towns mushroom, railways and roads are built, new industries and commercial activities set up. The whole environmental and economic scene changes and there are both winners and losers.

D Carajás company mining town

Statistics

	UK	ITALY	BRAZIL	JAPAN	INDIA
Total area (km²)	244 100	301 270	8 511 965	377 801	3 287 260
Total population (millions)	58.3	57.2	159.1	125.2	943.0
Population density: people per km²	241	194	19	332	317

Population

	UK	ITALY	BRAZIL	JAPAN	INDIA
Birth rate per 1000 people	14	11	26	10	31
Death rate per 1000 people	12	11	8	6	10
Life expectancy (male and female)	73M 79F	73M 80F	64M 69F	76M 83F	60M 61F
Fertility (children per female)	2	1	3	2	4
Population structure 0–14 15–59 60+	19% 60% 21%	17% 63% 20%	35% 58% 7%	19% 64% 17%	37% 56% 7%
Urban population	89%	67%	76%	77%	26%

Environment and economy

	UK	ITALY	BRAZIL	JAPAN	INDIA
Rate of urban growth per year	0.3%	0.6%	2.3%	0.6%	2.9%
Land use: arable grass forest	27% 46% 10%	31% 17% 23%	7% 22% 58%	11% 2% 67%	56% 4% 23%
% of workforce in: farming industry services	2 28 70	9 32 59	25 25 50	7 34 59	62 11 27
GNP per person (US$)	$17 970	$19 620	$2 920	$31 450	$290
Unemployment	9.4%	11.6%	5.9%	3.0%	n/a
Energy used (tonnes/person/year)	5.40	4.02	0.44	4.74	0.35

Society and quality of life

	UK	ITALY	BRAZIL	JAPAN	INDIA
Infant mortality (deaths per 1000 births)	8	9	57	5	88
People per doctor	300	211	1000	600	2439
Food supply (calories per person per day)	3317	3561	2824	2903	2395
Adult literacy	99%	97%	81%	99%	50%
TVs per 1000 people	434	421	207	613	35
Aid received or given per person	$50 given	$53 given	$1.2 received	$90 given	$1.7 received
Education spending (% of GNP)	5.3	4.1	n/a	5.0	3.5
Military spending (% of GNP)	4.0	2.0	n/a	1.0	2.5
United Nations Human Development Index (out of 1.0)	0.92	0.91	0.80	0.94	0.44

Figures are for 1992–95. Source: *Philip's Geographical Digest* (United Nations, World Bank). The Human Development Index is worked out by the UN. It is a summary of national income, life expectancy, adult literacy and education. It is a measure of human progress. In 1992, HDI ranged from 0.21 to 0.94.

General

Longest river: Amazon (6280km)
Highest mountain: Pico da Bandeira (2890m)
Largest city: São Paulo (16.4 million)
Capital: Brasília (1.59 million)
Languages: Portuguese
Currency: Real
Religion: Roman Catholic (87%),
Protestant (8%)

Access to safe water and sanitation 1990-96 (%)

	Safe water	Sanitation
Brazil	73	44
UK	99	99
USA	99	99

Social

Media and communications – 1994 (per 100 people)

	Newspapers	Radios	TVs	Computers
Brazil	5	39	25	0.9
UK	35	142	45	15.2
USA	23	212	78	29.8

Inequality

Real GDP per head (US $)

	Brazil	UK	USA
Richest 20%	18 563	36 164	51 705
Poorest 20%	578	3963	5800

Recent trends

Brazil		UK		USA	
1980	1994	1980	1994	1980	1994
HDI changes					
0.673	0.783	0.892	0.913	0.905	0.942
GDP per person (US$)					
2049	1993	10 161	13 132	16 389	20 500

Economic

Poverty

Region	People in poverty (%)
South-East	13
South	17
North	28
Centre West	29
North-East	45

Tourism (1993)

	Brazil	UK	USA
Foreign tourists	1 650 000	19 488 000	45 779 000
US $ spent	1 449 000	13 451 000	57 621 000

Glossary

aborigine the first people to settle an area

absolute poverty lacking basic needs like water, food, shelter, clothing and education

agribusiness farming and processing carried out world-wide by large-scale multinational companies

ALADI a trading partnership between Latin American countries that are not members of MERCOSUL

bio-diversity the range of different species found in an area

boulevard a tree-lined straight avenue

caatinga dry, scrub vegetation which grows in north-east Brazil

Candomblé a spirit religion which originates from the Yoruba people of Nigeria

capital money available for investment and not needed for everyday expenses

citadel area surrounded by defences

company town town built, owned and maintained by a company

core an area of concentrated economic activity, development and usually wealth

decentralize move activities and control of activities from one centre to many other locations

ecologist someone who studies the links between living things, and between living things and the environment

ecosystem a set of links between vegetation, climate and other parts of the environment

environmentalist a person who studies and cares for the environment

EU European Union

exploitation using other people for your own profit

favela informal settlement, often of squatters in home-made houses

favelados people who live in *favelas*

fazenda plantation or large farm specializing in one or more crops

garden city town planned to include trees, lawns, parks and flowers within the urban area

garimpeiros gold miners

greenhouse effect the global warming of the atmosphere caused probably by the increase in carbon dioxide in the air

IMF International Monetary Fund international organization which uses funds from wealthy nations to encourage and control economic growth in the Third World

indigenous people the first people to settle an area

industrial heartland central area of growth, investment and increasing production

inflation increase in prices and fall in the value of money

infrastructure the networks and systems that join areas together and allow resources, ideas and people to move between them

integrated steelworks steelworks which carries out all the processes of production from iron ore to high quality steel on one site

intensive high inputs of labour and/or capital to increase production

labour the workers or work-force

latifundios very large farms owned by big companies or wealthy families, many of whom have owned them since colonial times

MERCOSUL trading block with special agreements formed by Brazil, Argentina, Paraguay and Uruguay

micro-region small area with its own characteristics, which works as a unit

municipality city council

natural increase increase in population caused by more births than deaths

newly industrialized country (NIC) country which has recently changed its economy from mainly agricultural to mainly industrial and commercial

OPEC Organization of Petroleum Exporting Countries

peripheral area away from core areas where development is slower

pistoleiros gunmen

plateau flat upland area

pioneer fringe boundary area between colonized and uncolonized land

potential evapotranspiration the amount of rainfall necessary to allow for evaporation and release of water by plants and still leave a surplus

real GDP (real gross domestic product) total production of a country, measured in US dollars, but adjusted to take into account the cost of living in the country concerned

redevelop replace existing buildings etc, with new ones

savanna tropical grassland, often with scattered trees

sertao dry land with sparse thorny vegetation and grasses; also wilderness

sharecropper farmer who rents land but pays the farmer with a share of the crops grown

subsidies money given out, usually by governments, to reduce prices on certain things, e.g. food, farm produce

temperate with mild temperatures

TNC (transnational corporation) business which operates globally and has decision making managers in several countries

urban realms large areas of urban residential land outside the city centre, with their own large retail and leisure facilities

urbanization increase in the proportion of the total population living in towns, and therefore the growth of towns

Varzea flood plains in Amazonia, usually with black, fertile, silty soils and dense vegetation

Bibliography

Brazilian Embassy, *Brazil in the School* (1996)

BBC, *Brazil 2000* (video) (1996)

Buckle,y R, 'Amazonia, an ecological crisis', *Understanding Global Issues*, 2/92, European Schoolbooks Publishing Ltd (1992)

Caipora Women's Group, *Women in Brazil*, Latin American Bureau (1993)

Development Education Centre (Birmingham), *Fala Favela* (photopack), DEC(Bhm) (1990)

Dimenstein, G, *Brazil: war on children*, Latin American Bureau (1991)

Huckle, J, 'Brazil', *Unit 5: What we consume*, Global environmental Education Programme, WWF (1988)

MacDonald, N, *Brazil: a mask called progress*, Oxfam (1991)

Marshall, D, *Brazil*, Heinemann (1994)

McCarthy, S, *In search of El Dorado*, Trocaire (1996)

Reed, A, *Brazil: issues in development*, Unwin Hyman (1989)

Trocaire, *Views from Brazil*, DEC (Birmingham) (1990)

Vallely, P, *Promised Lands*, Christian Aid (1992)

Index